T0207578

If God Were in
Charge of Church!

*How the "One Way" Path to Jesus
Has Taken 41,000 Broken Trails*

PASTOR KENDALL L. HALL

WESTBOW
PRESS®
A DIVISION OF THOMAS NELSON
& ZONDERVAN

WestBow Press books may be ordered through booksellers or by contacting:

WestBow Press
A Division of Thomas Nelson & Zondervan
1663 Liberty Drive
Bloomington, IN 47403
www.westbowpress.com
844-714-3454

ISBN: 978-1-6642-0987-9 (sc)
ISBN: 978-1-6642-0988-6 (e)

Library of Congress Control Number: 2020920738

Print information available on the last page.

WestBow Press rev. date: 10/23/2020

To my wife, Sharon Bonita. I could not imagine walking forward in any ministry without my powerful prayer warrior. Her encouragement to my heart and her sometimes foot to my bottom keep me moving in the right direction. She never had to tell you she was a Christian—she showed you she was one.

This book is dedicated to her.

> Brethren, if anyone among you wanders from the truth, and someone turns him back, let him know that he who turns a sinner from the error of his way will save a soul from death and cover a multitude of sins. (James 5:19–20)

Contents

Introduction

I feel I need to wax philosophical for just a moment, if I could.

Who are we? Who are you? I can say with all certainty that we are the sum of all those who have gone before us. Is my very own blood mine, or am I simply the DNA of both my father and my mother? My DNA is a mixture of what once belonged to them, which they received from their parents, who received from their parents, and so on. The blood that flows with in my body is not totally mine, but a human potion that has been brewing for thousands of years. My own body is a mere hand-me-down.

To whom does my mind belong? Are my thoughts really mine, or are they an elixir that has been mixed for me by my experiences throughout my life? At birth, our minds are clean slates ready to be imprinted on by what we see, what we hear, and what we experience, as well as by the input of those we encounter throughout our time here on planet Earth.

Input from parents and siblings at a young age sets the base. General respect was taught by a firm and loving father. Compassion was shown and absorbed by a gracious and caring mother. Being a bully was not in my person before I was taught how to be one by an older and bigger brother. Demanding my rights as an individual was not known to me but was shown to me by and older sister in a discussion about needing her own private quarters away from my other two sisters.

Through elementary school, math and science were introduced into a curious mind, and so was socialization, which was being molded by outside influences. On the playground at recess, Billy thought a girl was cute, so my mind was introduced to girls in that way, and I began to think on the same terms. Through high school, I was shown how to pick cool friends and stay away from those who, as I was taught, were "losers."

Our minds and our opinions do not stop because we reach a certain age. Being out of high school does not mean my mind is full, I no longer need to learn, and I no longer need to be influenced. As a matter of fact, life itself is a continuous series of learning experiences until we go to be with the Lord.

Into my adulthood, my wife educated me on being in love. She said I can say that I love her, but she needed me to show her that I love her. This was a lesson that I thought I knew but needed to be reeducated on. It's amazing how just a few small flowers become a huge exclamation point to the statement "I love you."

As we grow, our views on life change, our views on politics change, our views on love change, and our views on religion change. I was born Catholic. Now I am a Protestant, and that came because I allowed myself to see the world through different eyes and, more important, different influences and scriptures.

I was raised Catholic in a loving home with good parents and loving siblings. Through fourth grade in Saint Francis Elementary School, all I knew of was popes, nuns, and beautiful statue-filled churches. I had no idea that there was such a thing as a Baptist church, Church of Christ, or Assembly of God. It wasn't until my mind was introduced to other thoughts on the issue of God that my brain had different options and thoughts to choose from.

Are these currently my original thoughts and ideas? Or are they a mixture of the thoughts and ideas given to me by all the steps taken in my life?

I am a pastor and teacher of God's Word, and I don't believe I have ever had an original thought concerning God. The science beaker that is my mind has continued to mix what Sister Marcia poured into me in second grade, stirred in with what Matthew Henry has added time and time again and what was contributed by John MacArthur, J. Vernon McGee, John Hagee, and others. It's mostly influenced by the writings of the apostles, Paul, Peter, John, and Daniel, Moses, and so on. Nothing original here, just carrying the torch.

And to be honest, there is nothing original in the thought to my mentors. Every thought they embarked on producing had its own beginning with the thoughts of others, save Paul, Peter, John, Daniel, and Moses, whose thoughts were the products of the Holy Spirit Himself. But even Paul, Peter, John, Daniel, and Moses had their own life experiences to mold how they perceived their thoughts. The originality that is the biblical writers has a lot to do with what and how they penned.

The point being is we are a sum of our experiences, good or bad, and our decisions and thoughts have come to the forefront of our minds through a well-traveled road. Not an original thought, just a pavement that life's experiences has poured. Filled with some smooth drives and some potholes. This is the basis of how we have learned church.

I have an older brother whom I love dearly. Just like every family with siblings, we find different ways to love each other, different ways to talk to each other, and different ways to disagree with each other. We seem to disagree on many fronts, and each of us hammers away at our points not to win our wars but to make our points. It's his life experiences versus mine. However, there is one thing about family: we don't quit on each other.

My brother (Catholic) and I (Baptist) howl, scream, yell, stomp, pout, cry, and generally disagree on most religious points, but we never end our conversations without telling each other that we love each other. That's family.

The element of disagreeing in love is missing in churches today. We use a phrase like "Agree to disagree" but don't really mean it. We do disagree with each other, with each side standing their ground, but we somehow stop short of finding out what God wants. I guess the statement is true that we do agree that we disagree. But do we disagree with each other, or are we disagreeing with God? He is the same yesterday, today, and forever whereas I am constantly changing. I guess the real question we should ask is, "Aren't we all supposed to be on the same page spiritually?"

I mean that as a legitimate question. Are we not the church? Aren't we all supposed to be in this one thing together? Why would we disagree on anything concerning God? And to agree to disagree? On what? How I view baptism, as opposed to how you view baptism? Music? Gifts? Why should we agree to disagree on anything concerning what is written in God's Bible?

During one of our sessions, my brother said, "You can worship God your way, and I will worship Him my way," and we left the conversation at that. I hear this statement, or others like it, so much that I started to accept it and tried to move on. *Sure, I* thought. *I will just worship Him the Protestant way, you can worship Him the Catholic way, and we will leave it at that.* We agreed to disagree, say "I love you," and end our talk.

This has bothered me for a long time because I do love my brother, and I see that although we agreed that he would worship God in his way and I would worship Him my way, my brother and I could never get to the point where we could worship God together. The reason for that is—are you ready for this?—church!

That's right, church! Men seem to be in charge of God's church and church has divided the worship of my brother and me. We agree to disagree on far too many points because the founders of my church says this, the founders of his church says that, and we are kept at a distance because of our religious differences. On the surface, agreeing to disagree may seem logical, but it is filled with division.

"You worship God your way, and I will worship Him my way" has become a mantra that divides believers far too long. The question isn't who's right or who's wrong, my way or your way. The question is, Why aren't we doing it His way, God's way? Why in the name of heaven can't we just sit down, open His Word, read scripture, say "Do it this way," and agree to agree that God Almighty is right?

The apostle Paul tells us that "Our struggle is not against flesh and blood, but against … spiritual forces of wickedness in the heavenly places" (Eph. 6:12). Satan's job is to confuse and divide, and he bombards believers with false doctrine, trying to confuse and distract them from biblical truth (Eph. 4:14). That is his job. I honestly believe that this is Satan's greatest victory: to divide the Church and believers. Paul said in 1 Corinthians 1:10, "Now I plead with you brethren, by the name of our Lord Jesus Christ, that you all speak the same thing, and that there be no divisions among you, but that you be perfectly joined together in the same mind and in the same judgment." At present, we are divided into broken, jagged pieces, each cutting at each other in the name of the church.

Agreeing to disagree has confused and divided believers, and put a different church building every other block, created division between good people, and separated God's people in the name of religion in a way that God never intended and never told us to do.

How many churches are there supposed to be in the world? If you said more than one, you would be wrong. There is the Church that Jesus spoke of in Matthew 16, and that is the only one there is supposed to be. Why do we have more than one church? Because men get in the way and want to run things. Men take charge in the name of God. There is Judaism, of course, and there will always be Judaism, but there is only suppose to be one Church.

If I were to ask you to take a guess as to how many Christian denominations there are in the world, how many would you guess? No, I am not talking how many churches or church buildings. Let me give you some help. I am Baptist, and as far as Baptist Christian denominations, we have Southern Baptist, Northern Baptist, Independent Baptist, Bible Baptist, Freewill Baptist, Primitive Baptist, Old Regular Baptist, Reformed Baptist, Seven Day Baptist ... There are over one hundred different Baptist denominations alone. So taking that into consideration, how many different Christian denominational followings are there?

If there are over one hundred different Baptist followings, then there are Catholic, Lutheran, Church of God, Church of Christ, Pentecostal, Assembly of God, Methodist, Presbyterian, and more. You would have to guess the denominations are at least in the hundreds, maybe in the (dare I say) thousands. Maybe they're in the (oh, boy, don't say it) tens of thousands?

According to Wikipedia, there are more than forty-one thousand different Christian denominations. Let me repeat it so you know it is not an error: forty-one thousand! A four, a one, and three zeros. How many are there supposed to be? One! How much more agreeing to disagreeing can we do?

When men get involved, we can take one church and fracture it into forty-one thousand different pieces, with all claiming to be the only way to God. It is as if God has become the peanut butter that gets spread over forty-one thousand different types of bread crying out for their own specific types of jellies and jams, all the while feeding very few.

Is this okay? Can this be all right to a holy God who claims to be a jealous God and wants it His way and His way only? Can there be a God to the Baptist, another God to the Catholics, and then the Pentecostals, Lutherans, et cetera? The Church of Jesus Christ is in a battle, and we cannot watch from the sidelines. I remember the words to a song from Beloved called "Death to Traitors," which says,

> We were born for battle, without vision we will die.
> We were born for battle, against the tide of compromise.

We cannot go with the flow and compromise on the Church in the name of organized religion. We must be equipped to fight the good fight that we were born to fight.

The question is this: Have we let the some of the experiences and thoughts of every person become our reasoning for what a church should be? Humans have broken the church into forty-one thousand pieces, but what if God were in charge of the church today? What would it be like not only to you and I, but what would the church be like for Him?

Chapter 1

Who Do You Say That I Am?

I love the fact that God allows me to see His Son in everything I do, and this time was no different. My wife had decided that she wanted us to update our kitchen and bring it into the twenty-first century with a new countertop. Her younger sister decided to update the kitchen in her own house, and my wife felt that it was a great idea. There was not any competition between two loving sisters; it was simply time to update the kitchen.

My wife left it up to me, her trusted steed, to research granite countertops, and I had to find out everything there is to know about them so she could decide what to get. I felt it was best to seek wise council, so I found a man who is a professional in our area, and he educated me on the matters and nuances of granite countertops.

I knew exactly what my wife meant by research. My job was to find out as much as I could about granite. However, I wasn't to pick out a design, color, or price; I was to find out what granite is. With the help of my expert, I was taught that a granite countertop is indeed rock.

My first question to the professional granite dealer and installer was, "Are there different kinds of granite?" I asked if there was one kind of granite that was better than others. Maybe one was stronger or better suited for a kitchen. He informed me about granite in the most simplistic of terms. He told me that all granite countertops are rock. A granite countertop is a rock that has been cut and polished in such a way that it could be sold at top dollar and possibly please my wife. Maybe.

I was surprised by the simplicity with which this man spoke. Just a rock? How can that be when there is store after store, salesperson after salesperson, and myriads of different kinds of granite countertops to choose from? Just a rock? I didn't believe it.

It's true: granite is just a rock.

The truth of the matter is this: One supplier will brag that their polished rock is better than the next supplier in the hope that you will pay them more money than the next one, because my wife must have a better piece of polished rock than her sister.

Which brings me to this point: The simple beauty is that the rock has been polished and cut and is sold on every corner by competing and greedy salespeople to appease buyers.

My wife followed her sister's idea for a new kitchen because her sister liked the kitchen in a friend's house. Her friend saw this new kitchen in a popular magazine that displayed a woman's house in California, and I am sure the mystery woman saw a kitchen in a magazine or movie, a friend's house, or something else.

It appears that since Adam and Eve, humans have accepted things and ideas that the people around them and in their society accept—for no other reason than because society has accepted it. Adam ate from the tree because Eve ate, and as a society, we go along with the status quo. We are born followers. This is not a slight against humans, just a fact. We are told, in no uncertain terms, to follow Jesus because we are followers who need direction (Matt. 4:19).

Problems arise when we follow people instead of Jesus. We follow others, and we somehow feel that if enough people do something, it must be right and okay to do. We follow the path that others have blazed, sometimes not even caring about which direction it may take us.

For instance, as a society we know that smoking and chewing tobacco is bad, yet tobacco remains a billion-dollar industry. Smoking is harmful, and there are very few people in our society who say that smoking and chewing tobacco is a good and right thing, yet society encourages it by its mere allowance of it.

There is a push to legalize marijuana and other drugs. The argument is that if we legalize it, there will be less crime, and we can tax it and produce revenue. The truth is that according to bjs. gov, 80 percent of all prison inmates have had or have a current drug problem. Out of all prison inmates, 60 percent were on drugs at their arrest. (So much for deterring crime.) The revenue generated would either go back into regulating it or into the pockets of shady politicians.

As a society, we follow, and we feel that if we accept something, it must be all right. That mentality is also prevalent in the church. I was talking to my wife, Sharon, about how we do things in the church because we can justify them to ourselves. We often think that if we are all right with something, then God is all right with it, and we don't look to find out what is in the forefront of God's mind on the issue through His scripture.

Sharon said that if God knows our hearts and our intentions, then that alone should be all that matters. I disagree. For a long time now, the church has accepted things in the name of "good intentions," which are more damaging than drugs and tobacco. Yes, God does know our hearts, and that should frighten us. We mostly have a heart for ourselves and a heart of disobedience for not following His Word.

I was thinking of the Shema from Deuteronomy 6:4, a prayer recited twice a day that serves as a centerpiece of the morning and evening Jewish prayer services, which says, "Hear, Israel, the Lord is our God, the Lord is One." When I was dwelling on this prayer, I wondered why we have so many different churches when there is only one God.

A search on Wikipedia says that there are forty-one thousand different Christian denominations in the world. There are forty-one thousand different ways of how to go to what the Shema calls the one Lord, our God. This is what happens when people take charge of the church that Jesus began.

A little more research showed that the smallest state in the United States is Rhode Island, and the smallest city in Rhode Island is North Providence, which is 1.29 square miles. I counted twenty-one churches in the smallest city in the smallest state in our union. That would be one church building every half a mile. There are many, many churches.

I live in Jonesboro, Louisiana, and I can stand on a certain spot on the road and see one Southern Baptist church building to my left and another to my right. We have thirty-one Baptist churches in our small phone book.

There are many Baptist churches—Southern Baptist, Missionary Baptist, Freewill Baptist, Northern Baptist. Not to mention Catholic, Church of God, Church of Christ, Pentecostal, Full Gospel, Methodist, Jehovah's Witnesses, and Mormons.

Many, many churches, all professing to serve one Lord and God. All professing to serve Jesus Christ in one way or another. Why so many? If we indeed serve only one God, why so many churches? Why? Has God changed? Is He now the peanut butter that needs to be spread over forty-one thousand different types of bread? Is He creamy for us and chunky for them? Why so many churches?

I have to say right now that I am not asking churchgoers to stop going to their local church on Sunday, Wednesday, or any other time. I am saying that there cannot be forty-one thousand different paths to Christ, and we should look for reasons to band together in unity in His name. Baptists joined with Catholics, joined with Lutherans, joined with Pentecostals—all in the name of Jesus. The second greatest commandment is to love your neighbor as yourself, and you may have to leave the comfort of your denomination to do that.

I have found that the answer to most difficult problems usually starts with a good question. I believe that the answer to why there are so many churches starts with this question: Who do you say Jesus is? it is a fair question because, after all, we are His church. There cannot be forty-one thousand different answers to that question. There can only be one answer.

Jesus asked His disciple a question in Matthew 16:13–14. "When Jesus came into the region of Caesarea Philippi, He asked His disciples, saying, 'Who do men say that I, the Son of Man, am?' So they said, 'Some say John the Baptist, some Elijah, and others Jeremiah or one of the prophets.'"

Jesus answered His own question when He asked who people say the Son of Man is. Jesus claimed to be the Son of Man but asked His disciples who other men thought He was. He asked His followers that question two thousand years ago, and He is still asking people that same question today.

Mormons and Jehovah's Witnesses believe that Jesus was, more or less, an elevated man. He was a man who had some of the attributes of God, or at least was a godly man, or was a prophet— but they do not believe that Jesus Christ was the Creator, God, in the flesh. Jesus made His claims to deity in John chapters 8, 10, and 14, but so many people have other views on who they think the Son of Man is. As a matter of fact, from the official site about Mormonism, I got this: "While we do not believe the Bible to be inerrant, complete or the final word of God …" When you see the Bible as incomplete and a book with errors, it doesn't matter what Jesus claimed to be, just who you might say He is.

Mormons do have extra writings, the Book of Mormon and the Great Pearls of Wisdom, and they can write more if they believe the Bible is in error or incomplete, or God may need their help with an extra book or two. Jehovah's Witnesses have gone so far as to write their own translation of the Bible, in what is call the New World Translation, and their followers are told not to read out of any other translation but their own so they can be led down a path determined by their leaders, who are men, either right or wrong.

This comes from the official Jehovah's Witness website: "However, we take Jesus at his word when he said: 'The Father is greater than I am.' (John 14:28) So we do not worship Jesus, as we do not believe that he is Almighty God." To the Jehovah's Witnesses, Jesus is not worthy of worship.

So who do they say Jesus is? To the Mormons and Jehovah's Witnesses, He is who they want Him to be. Both would say that Jesus is the Christ, or who they think the Christ ought to be, but both stop short of saying that He is indeed God in flesh or that Jesus is who we are to worship. To the Mormons and Jehovah's Witnesses, Jesus is merely an example to follow. This is the opinion of men.

Jesus turned His question from the opinion of men to the thoughts of His disciples. Jesus asked in Matthew 16:15, "But who do you say that I am?" That is the question for all ages. Who do you say He is? Do you hang on to what is recited daily in Israel, that the Lord your God is one God? Or do you follow men who may think that Jesus was just a real good guy, and we should be more like Him?

With forty-one thousand churches around, could He be forty-one thousand different versions of who I think He is? Do you buy into the thought that he is the God of the Baptist, and then another God to the Catholics, and yet another God to the Charismatic, and then maybe the Mormons and Jehovah's Witnesses?

With forty-one thousand different churches in the world professing Jesus Christ, can all of them be right? Can every building on every corner have its own version of the one Lord and God? Can there be forty-one thousand different paths to Jesus?

Of a recent survey I found, 26 percent of Christians surveyed do not believe that Jesus was the Son of God but feel that He was a good teacher who embodied Godly characteristics. That would seem to be the thought of the Mormons and Jehovah Witnesses: a Godly example to follow, but not God.

Also, 64 percent of these Christians believe that the Bible is real, whereas over 30 percent feel it is metaphorical and allegory, meaning that the Bible is just a bunch of philosophical stories that mean one thing to me and then one thing to you, so truth becomes relevant to the hearer.

If we see the Word of God as metaphors and allegories, as mere stories and examples to follow, we are forced to use our own minds as a filter to determine what God really means. In essence, we are reduced to having God run His Word by us for our interpretation and final approval.

I see that this is where the problems begin. Most seem to want to put the Bible in their own words or their own beliefs while not really digging into the Word to see what it really says or means. Jeremiah 17:9 states, "The heart is deceitful above all things, And desperately wicked." By our very nature, humans are deceitful

7

and wicked, so if humans try to interpret God and His Word, when we want to put things in our own words and opinions, by nature it will come out deceitful and wicked. How can a deceitful and wicked bunch like us be the final approval of the words of a holy God?

Having said that, I find that people search for churches that meet their own personal needs, putting themselves above what is written and their personal needs above seeking truth. Far too many people already have a set of beliefs, and then they search out a church that agrees with those beliefs. Most go to church out of duty, tradition, or because it is close to their house. Finding a church where the truth and scripture are being emphasized does not seem to be the driving factor of church attendance.

People attend church for every reason under the sun: "This is where we have always gone." "I like the people here." "My wife makes me go." We attend church for many reasons—out of duty, religion, family, or tradition—with every church on every corner professing that it is true to God and His Word. Can forty-one thousand different travelers going down forty-one thousand paths all be going in the same right direction?

A friend of mine who is a deacon in a large church recently came under fire because of a scriptural stance he took. His church didn't like the fact that he pointed out a couple troublemakers in the church. He felt that due to his position as deacon, and the fact that we are told in Romans 16:17 to "note those who cause divisions and offenses, contrary to the doctrine which you learned, and avoid them," he should speak up. Some others in that church felt he should not have named names and treated him harshly because of it.

He had attended this church his entire life, but he and his wife were considering leaving this big church that his grandparents founded and his parents had raised him in because there was no leader or leadership, and people were attacking each other in the name of God.

He told me he was going to shop around and look for a new church (Baptist, of course). I told him that the preacher at another church close to him (Baptist, of course) less than one mile from his home was a good teacher. I told him that he would get fed there and the people who attended were good people. He said he knew of that church, their leader, and their people, and he friend told me, "I would never step foot in that church!"

So much for "Love thy neighbor."

He had been hurt before by some member in the past. It didn't seem to be about getting fed spiritually to him. It didn't seem to be about finding God's truth or His will. It turned into finding a church where people had not hurt him before and where he might feel comfortable. I can't recall a scripture where we are told to feel comfortable in our walk with God.

It seemed that to my friend, past hurts and past experience had everything to do with searching out a church. If there were a few past hurts with people in his present church, or a few hurts in a future church, he wouldn't attend. Are we not told in Matthew 5:23–24, "Therefore if you bring your gift to the altar, and there remember that your brother has something against you, leave your gift there before the altar, and go your way. First be reconciled to your brother, and then come and offer your gift"?

Matthew 5:23–24 is an easy solution to confront those who have hurt you, but it is difficult to practice. It is much easier to leave a building on this corner and go to another building, as long as there is no one in that building who has hurt you before. The mantra becomes "I will follow God to your church as long as I like it there and no one hurts my feelings or disagrees with me there."

Casting Crowns says in a song, "If we are the body, why aren't our hands reaching?" Are we one body? If we are one body, we should look out for each other. It is like having a hangnail on our big toe that bothers us and sometimes will fester, but instead of dealing with the toe, we would much rather amputate the entire foot than to come to terms with the infected digit.

(Just to give you an update, my friend and his wife currently still have their frustrated and bruised egos in the church building that his forefathers founded.)

What keeps a person in a certain church building? I had this conversation with a woman many years ago. I had listened to her pastor speak before, and I had true scriptural concerns that she wasn't getting fed in the church she was attending. I asked her whether she felt that her pastor correctly handled the Word. She said that she attended that particular church because every Easter and Christmas, they had a concert cantata, and she loved to sing in the choir. It didn't matter to her what the man in the pulpit was saying as long as she could sing in the choir.

I think the question to "Who do you say that I am?" has a lot to do with why you go to church. Do you think Jesus is the divine brick mason whom we must keep too because the mortar of a particular building has the sweat and blood of a distant relative in it? Do you think that He is the great choir director who wants you to stand and sing?

I have always considered myself a good teacher, and like every good teacher, there is a pop quiz now and then. Here is my first pop quiz to my students reading this book.

Pop Quiz: Why do you go to church? Why?

Let me give you a bit of my testimony. I used to be ashamed of my past when I had to bring it to certain church followers. I was born into a Catholic home and attended a Catholic school through the fourth grade. My father died a professing Catholic, and my mother is still devout. I was raised to observe holy water, genuflect in church, and pray to saints.

In my early twenties, I followed a young lady into a nondenominational Charismatic church with an emphasis on spiritual gifts. This was my first experience away from the Catholic Church, and it frightened me in many ways. I didn't know how to take the high emotions, heartfelt music, or speaking in ecstatic language. This was so different than the Catholic Church I grew up in as a small boy. I was finding God at two different ends of the spectrum.

The leadership in this nondenominational church had a falling out, and a church split occurred. I was a Christian baby at the time, and I followed some mentors of mine and others into an Assembly of God church. My friends tried to explain the dangers of a nondenominational church. They said that when one person is in control, many problems can happen. I didn't see that as clearly as I do now, but I followed them. I became a card-carrying member of the Assembly of God for years and even got baptized there (full submersion, of course).

Three different churches early in my walk, and all three seemed uniquely different. The Assembly of God and the nondenominational church had similarities, but I couldn't help but feel that each church felt that the others were doing wrong.

Now, I am in a Southern Baptist church because this is where God put me, doing things different that the others before. I used to be ashamed to tell good Baptist people my past, but God has shown me that I have a unique perspective when it comes to doing church. I don't have to read about it—I lived and experienced it.

Although confused on many issues at the time, God has showed me His truths through scripture. Through my path, I can understand the mindset of praying to saints and transubstantiation. Through my path, I can understand the desire to feel God through the gifts of the Spirit. My path has given me a better understanding of many things.

1. How people will trust and follow people.
2. How people don't know they are misled.
3. How Satan uses church and religion to lead people away from God.
4. How proper study of the Bible is the only hope for truth and freedom in Christ.

Forty-one thousand different followings. When I first started attending a Baptist church, I thought that there was such a thing as a "Back-Row" Baptist and a "Pot-Luck" Baptist. It seemed that the same people always sat in the back, and every time we got together, we ate. Maybe there are really forty-thousand and two different followings.

Jesus asked His disciples who they thought He was, and it was answered in Matthew 16:17. "Simon Peter answered and said, 'You are the Christ, the Son of the living God.'" And of course, that is the answer.

But the answer Peter gave was just the beginning. Matthew 16:18–19 states, "Jesus answered and said to him, 'Blessed are you, Simon Bar-Jonah, for flesh and blood has not revealed this to you, but My Father who is in heaven. And I also say to you that you are Peter, and on this rock I will build My church, and the gates of Hades shall not prevail against it.'"

"You are the Christ, the Son of the living God." This is the Church!

This small bit of information that Peter gave by the power of the Holy Spirit is what Jesus has built His Church on. This is the first mention of the Church in the Bible, and it is not in response as to where to worship. It is not in response to where to meet. It is not in response to where to eat. It is not in response to where to find people who like me. It is not in response to where I pray, sing, kneel, and tithe. The Church is the fact that Jesus is the Christ, the Son of the living God. This is the Church!

I hope we can all realize that a church building has never saved anyone. My friend always tells me that going into a church makes you a Christian just like standing under a carport makes you a car. Jesus, being the Christ, the Son of the Living God, is who saves people. If the church is this wonderful bit of information, if the Church is Jesus the Christ, how did we arrive at forty-one thousand different churches? Can there be forty-one thousand different versions of the Christ?

History shows us that early in the Church, there was indeed one church. Acts 2 begins with saying that the Church, the disciples of Jesus, were "all with one accord in one place." I don't believe that we have all been in one accord since. The biblical Church is people who hang on to the fact that Jesus is the Christ, the Son of God. The Church is people, you and I, and all who believe that Jesus is the Son of God. We are supposed to be in one accord about this. The Church is not our buildings and denominations.

After the first time *Church* is mentioned in Matthew 16, it is mentioned seventy-seven times in the New Testament, and in seventy times it is referred to as *the* Church. Not many individual churches, but one identity. There are not supposed to be forty-one thousand different churches. Beloved, we are not supposed to have even two different churches. The church is one body.

When Paul writes to the Corinthians, he entitles the letter, "To *the* church of God which is at Corinth," and when he writes to the Thessalonians, he says, "To *the* church of the Thessalonians." These are not buildings but people. In Colossians 1:24, Paul says, "I now rejoice in my sufferings for you, and fill up in my flesh what is lacking in the afflictions of Christ, for the sake of His body, which is *the* church."

Pop Quiz: What is the Church? The answer is His body.

I want to look at what Paul says in 1 Corinthians 12:7, "But the manifestation of the Spirit is given to each one for the profit of all." Verses 12–14 state, "For as the body is one and has many members, but all the members of that one body, being many, are one body, so also is Christ. For by one Spirit we were all baptized into one body—whether Jews or Greeks, whether slaves or free—and have all been made to drink into one Spirit. For in fact the body is not one member but many."

The Spirit was given to profit how many? All! And the body is one but has many members—not buildings, not factions, not followings, not denominations. We are baptized into how many bodies? One! The church is the members in the one body of Jesus. That Jesus is the Christ!

In 1 Corinthians 12:20 it says, *"But now indeed there are many members, yet one body."* Many members, not buildings, not followings, not opinions—one body that believes Jesus is the Christ, the Son of the living God. Not the Catholic version, not the Assembly of God, not Jehovah's Witnesses, not Mormon, and not the Baptist version of Christ, the Son of the living God.

Then there is 1 Corinthians 12:28. "And God has appointed these in THE church: first apostles, second prophets, third teachers, after that miracles, then gifts of healings, helps, administrations, varieties of tongues."

God has appointed in the Church. Not your local church, and then their local church over there, and then some in that local church over there. God has built His Church on the fact that Jesus is the Christ, the Son of the living God.

Where did we go wrong?

There is only one question: Who do you say the Son of man is? If you have filled out a membership card … If you have walked the aisle … If you were sprinkled or baptized … If you attend church three times a week … If you exercise spiritual gifts … If you teach Sunday school or sing in the choir … All those things have their place, but they are the wrong answers to who Jesus is. The only answer is that Jesus is the Christ, your Savior.

With men taking their opinions, disagreements, interpretations, and inflated egos into doing God's will, one church can quickly be broken up into forty-one thousand different pieces of polished rock, with each man trying to sell his on a street corner. I can't think of anything that pleases Satan more than us divided. There has to come a time when we take the hands of men off the steering wheel and let God take control once again. The truth is that currently, humans are in charge of the forty-one thousand different churches, and God is in charge of the one true Church that believes Jesus is the Christ, the Son of the living God.

I am reminded of the words of the apostle Paul in Philippians 2:2, "fulfill my joy by being like-minded, having the same love, being of one accord, of one mind." I believe it would fulfill the joy of God too.

So the question is this: If God were in charge of the church, what would it be like?

Chapter 2

The Ground Rules

I seem to enjoy a passage more when I take into account the setting, period, and intent of the passage as well as the emotions. When I read the words of Christ in a red letter version of the Bible, I can't help but see the face of Jesus as He gives His words of wisdom to those who are seated near Him and listen intently. I imagine a sparkle in His eyes and His robes moving in the breeze, a child in hand, as He makes His point. I see the looks on the faces of the disciples as they receive His message and finally get the point. I guess that like all readers, I try to physically put myself there with the followers.

I remember every time I read "The Sermon on the Mount" in Matthew 5. I put myself on the hillside with the apostles, disciples, countless followers, and listeners, I am fixated and the words of Jesus, and I see His face in my mind's eye as He talks of those who are blessed.

"And seeing the multitudes, he went up on mountain: and when he was seated, his disciples came unto him: And he opened his mouth, and taught them" (Matt. 5:1–2).

I can see Him standing on the hillside, patiently waiting for people to get comfortable on the ground. A gentle breeze cools as it moves the tall grass on what I would imagine is a common hot day in Israel. I see in my mind's eye His disciples acting like ushers, seating people as they get set and look to the Master for direction. Jesus takes a comfortable seat Himself as He begins to teach them the things concerning His Father's kingdom.

"Blessed *are* the poor in spirit: for theirs is the kingdom of heaven. Blessed *are* they that mourn: for they shall be comforted" (Matt. 5:3–4).

As Jesus gives His opening remarks of those who will be blessed, I see Him patiently waiting as He looks into the eyes of those hungry and faithful. If the listeners are like I am, they hang on every word given by the Master and lean in closer, not wanting to miss a word as the voice of Jesus reaches them.

"Blessed *are* the meek: for they shall inherit the earth. Blessed *are* they which do hunger and thirst after righteousness: for they shall be filled. Blessed *are* the merciful: for they shall obtain mercy. Blessed *are* the pure in heart: for they shall see God" (Matt. 5:6–8).

As He rises to His feet, the grass under the sandals of Jesus is matted down, and I see Him walking in a central location giving His Father's list of blessings to a group that has been beaten down by Rome. Now, His followers hear the long-awaited words: that their God has blessings waiting for them. I can see Jesus with a sure look in His eyes and a smile on His face as He assures the listeners.

"Blessed *are* the peacemakers: for they shall be called the children of God" (Matt. 5:9).

Children of God. There cannot be a better title for people who live in this world. With His calm demeanor and sure words, Jesus instructs, educates, and encourages with the peace that only He can give.

I see the sun high in the sky, the gentle breeze cooling the day, and Jesus with a calm sureness expressing the Father's love and blessings. I see the faithful people seated in tall grass welcoming His words with open hearts, and I see a serene, peaceful, and utopian like pasture enjoyed by all.

> Blessed *are* those who are persecuted for righteousness' sake, for theirs is the kingdom of heaven. Blessed are you when they revile and persecute you, and say all kinds of evil against you falsely for My sake. Rejoice and be exceedingly glad, for great *is* your reward in heaven, for so they persecuted the prophets who were before you. You are the salt of the earth; but if the salt loses its flavor, how shall it be seasoned? It is then good for nothing but to be thrown out and trampled underfoot by men. You are the light of the world. (Matt. 5:10–14)

I see those who had been beaten down and persecuted for so long now sitting and listening eagerly. I see them encouraged that even though they will be persecuted more, they will be blessed. I see Jesus telling them this with a sureness, confidence, and loving smile that only our Lord and Master can give.

What I never seem to picture in my mind when I read Matthew 5 is Jesus starting His message with a joke or walking with incense lit as He passes through the crowd speaking in Latin. I don't see in my mind's eye our Lord passing back and forth, railing with a loud voice, pounding His Bible with His fist, and screaming at the top of His lungs to sell His view. I don't see the followers hearing the words of Jesus suddenly spinning in circles, jumping up and down, or falling on the ground without cause. And I don't see Jesus turning on the tears to make His point more believable just before He passes the offering plate for a building project.

I feel that the message Jesus gave has now been turned into a sellable item that needs to be palatable to the masses. The calm, measured, pointed message of Jesus Christ is now marketed like a ShamWow commercial, with people having to be sold on the concept of Jesus Christ (the Church) and what He should mean to them (the listeners). The words that have fallen dull to most now need to be propped up with a proper Sunday service, a well-timed scream, or a railing by a Sunday morning salesman, because we don't believe that doing it the way Jesus did it is effective any longer. Shame on us! Doing it the way Jesus did it should be rule number one. What happens when we do it our way?

If God were in charge of the Church, I am sure He would set some rules (which He has). We have a difficult time with rules, seeing how He gave Adam and Eve just one rule to follow (Don't eat …) and to us just ten (commandments) to start with, yet we couldn't keep up. Therefore, He tried to make it easier for us by saying, "If you can't keep the ten easy rules, can you keep up with two? Love God, and love your neighbor." If the Ten Commandments are "the Law," then Jesus gave us crib notes by telling us to just follow Deuteronomy 6:5 and Leviticus 19:18, love God and love your neighbor, respectively. These are easy rules to hear, but somehow they are difficult to follow.

If God were allowed to be in charge of the Church, He would have ground rules, and they are needed. If you read Matthew 5, you will see that Jesus gives ground rules. If you are poor in spirit, you will receive the kingdom. When you mourn, you will be comforted. Those are types of ground rules. Be poor and receive. Mourn and be comforted. I will be getting the ground rules from scripture, and I will follow them throughout this book. I am a simple man with a very simple mind, and I see things this simple way: If God says it, I believe it. If God doesn't say it … well, my mind is far too simple to follow the abstract.

There are a couple ground-rule scriptures that I will mention throughout this book, and I need to take the time to have them fully understood so we can move forward on sound footing. The first verse is Psalm 138:2, which says, "I will worship toward Your holy temple, And praise Your name For Your lovingkindness and Your truth; For You have magnified Your word above all Your name." I need us to start here because as it is written, God magnifies His Word above all, including His name! This is no small thing because we know that at the very mention of the name of Jesus, every knee shall bow and every tongue shall confess that He is Lord (Rom. 14; Phil. 2).

The New International Version puts it this way: "For you have so exalted your solemn decree that it surpasses your fame," and either in the NIV, the Authorized King James, or the New King James Version, Psalm 138:2 says that God lifts His Word above His very name. And why shouldn't He? Without the Word, we may very well have never heard of Jesus Christ. It is the Word that tells us of Adam and Eve, Moses, the Ten Commandments, the Psalms, Matthew, Mark, Luke, John, Revelation, Jesus, and His sacrifice on the cross. It is the Word that tells us of the God of creation, His mercy, and His forgiveness. The Word is exalted, and it is the Word that must be obeyed.

Deuteronomy 8:3 says, "He might make you know that man shall not live by bread alone; but man lives by every word that proceeds from the mouth of the LORD," and these are the same words that Jesus gave the devil during His forty days of fasting and temptation in Matthew 4. Jesus could have stood tall and yelled to the devil, "I'm the Man!" and cast the evil one out of His sight, but Jesus took the time to quote scripture. The scripture He quoted is that man lives by every word that proceeds out of the mouth of God. That statement by Moses in Deuteronomy 8 and Jesus in Matthew 4 show just how high God exalts and lifts His Word.

When I see an Old Testament verse quoted again in the New Testament, it draws my attention, and I pay stricter attention when I see Moses wrote it. That brings me this chapter's first pop quiz.

Pop Quiz: What is the first book of the Bible? (Hint: It is a trick question.)

The first book is (drumroll, please) … The Pentateuch! The Pentateuch, or the Torah as it is called by the Jewish people, is considered one book written by Moses that was broken down into Genesis, Exodus Deuteronomy, Leviticus, and Numbers. Early titles were "The Book of Moses" (Ezra 6:18; Neh. 13:1; 2 Chron. 35:12; 25:4; cf. 2 Kings 14:6) and "The Book of the Torah" (Neh. 8:3), which seems to be a contraction of a fuller name, "The Book of the Torah of God" (Neh. 8:8, 18; 10:29–30; cf. 9:3).

The point is that Moses sat and wrote one book that was broken into five scrolls, so when you read out of Genesis, or Numbers, or Deuteronomy, you are reading out of the first 'book' in the Bible, the Pentateuch, the starting point.

When I reminded you that Moses wrote in Deuteronomy 8:3 that man shall live by every word of God, this is one of the first things God had given us in His Word. In setting His ground rules for us to follow, God put right up front to live by *every* word that proceeds from His mouth. By this statement written by Moses, we see how high God exalts His Word.

Ground rule number one is that God's Word is exalted, or lifted up, even above His name. When we have are disagreements about church, we need not look any further than to say "It is written," because if it is written, it is elevated and exalted.

The next ground-rule verse we need to see is also in the "first" book, at Deuteronomy 4:2, which says, "You shall not add to the word which I command you, nor take from it, that you may keep

21

the commandments of the LORD your God which I command you." This seems like a very reasonable request from the Creator and Author of the book. Don't add to it, and don't take away from it. Have we kept this request? No. Not only have we not kept this command that He has commanded us to keep, but we have also added to or taken away from His Word to the tune of forty-one thousand different churches. There is only one way to do His book, and that is *His* way.

I said that when I see an Old Testament verse requoted in the New Testament it draws my attention, and this verse really should hit home. It is found in Revelation, and I want to set up this passage for us.

How you would finish the Bible? How would you finish your book if you were God? How would you do it? Would you finish with John 3:16, "For God so loved the world"? Would you end your book with 2 Timothy 4:2, "Preach the word! Be ready in season and out of season. Convince, rebuke, exhort, with all longsuffering and teaching"? That would be a good one to end on, wouldn't it? How about Mark 16:15, "And He said to them, 'Go into all the world and preach the gospel to every creature'"?

Pop Quiz: How would you end your book if you were God?

Revelation is twenty-two chapters long, with twenty-one verses in the last chapter. God says this with the last verse before He closes His book: "The grace of our Lord Jesus Christ *be* with you all. Amen" (Rev. 22:21). But just before He closes His book, He give us one final warning, one thing He wants us to take with us on our journey. Revelation 22:18–19 says this:

> For I testify to everyone who hears the words of the prophecy of this book: If anyone adds to these things, God will add to him the plagues that are written in this book; and if anyone takes away from the words of the book of this prophecy, God

shall take away his part from the Book of Life, from the holy city, and *from* the things which are written in this book.

Sound familiar? It should. This is taken from Deuteronomy 4:2, however John, through the Holy Spirit, has added a caveat to it.

I see Deuteronomy 4:2 as God being a loving parent who wants to protect His children with the warning "Don't mess with My Word. It's for your own good," just like a parent who warns his child not play with a mean dog because he might bite you. But just like most children who don't obey their parents and begin walking in the direction of the dog, a stricter warning is given. I see Revelation 22:18–19 as a parent who has warned his child to avoid that mean dog, but the child hasn't, and the parent must now warn his child, "Get away from that dog, and I mean it! Get away for it, or you will get a spanking!"

God said in Deuteronomy 4:2, "Don't mess with My Word," and in Revelation 22:18–19 He said, "Don't mess with My Word, and I am not kidding!" Of course, when our Father in heaven gives a spanking, it can be severe.

Think about all the ways God disciplines His children. None are as severe as when we add to or take from His Word. Nowhere else are we told things like "If you lie, I will kick you out of the kingdom," or "If you commit adultery, I will add plagues into your life." We are told that these are sins, but we can be forgiven of these sins. The sin of adding to or taking from God's Word is more grievous that all other sins.

Think also about this: If you read God's Word and, even with your best intentions, add to His Word with things like knocking on doors for salvation or praying to saints (sorry … I mean saints *not* in the Bible), He will (not can, but will) add the plagues in the Bible unto you. "All the plagues?" That is what He said, and that doesn't sound very appealing to this simple mind.

23

If you take away from the words of His book—such as thinking God is done with Israel and has turned His full attention to the church, for example—God has the right to remove your name from the book and the holy city. To me, believing His Word is the simplest thing to do. Simply follow what He has written. It is as easy as pie (or unleavened bread).

God holds the upkeep and consistency of His Word to a higher standard than all other sin. I can hear the words of John Mark Hall of Casting Crowns right now:

> Out of all the voices calling out to me,
> I will chose to listen and believe the Voice of Truth.

The Word of God is the only voice we should follow. Like the perfect cake recipe, don't add another egg or take away the sugar. It's perfect.

I can almost hear my critics now. "But, Brother Hall, isn't the Bible just how you interpret it?" If I had a quarter for every time I heard someone tell me, "It's how you interpret it," I would probably be driving a Lexus instead of my trusty 2000 Ford Ranger. "How you interpreted it" is wedged somewhere between "Agree to disagree" and "Under attack." The question is (and this is not a quiz), Do we have the right to interpret scripture? Do I have what it takes to read God's Word and say that it could mean one thing to me and another thing to you? With seven billion people in the world, can I read John 3:16, "For God so loved the world" in seven billion different ways?

Let's do a little math and add some scripture together so you will see the point about humans' ability. If Jeremiah 17:9 tells us, "The heart is deceitful above all things, And desperately wicked; Who can know it?" and Psalm 116:11 says, "All men are liars," and Paul echoes that thought in Romans 3:4, "let God be true but every man a liar," what that adds up to is that I am naturally deceitful and a hopeless liar with a wicked heart. If I were to be so bold as to think I could interpret scripture, it will come out of a deceitful, lying, and wicked heart because that is my nature. Why would I risk God's holy Word on that? Wouldn't I be best served to just read the Word, believe it, act on it, and be on my way?

Some may reply, "Well, I guess you could interpret it that way." And I do.

Here is a little more math for you: If God exalts His Word above His name, He tells us not to add to it or take from His Word, and we are deceitful, wicked, liars … If we add all that up, it comes out to the fact that humans cannot interpret scripture. We simply don't have what it takes in us.

But somehow I feel that even when I add up all the numbers about being able to interpret scripture, you still don't believe and see some adding errors my math. Please, If you can't believe my math, believe Peter.

> And so we have the prophetic word confirmed, which you do well to heed as a light that shines in a dark place, until the day dawns and the morning star rises in your hearts; knowing this first, that no prophecy of Scripture is of any private interpretation, for prophecy never came by the will of man, but holy men of God spoke as they were moved by the Holy Spirit. (2 Peter 1:19–21)

The word is *confirm* and you should heed it as a light in the dark world. No prophecy of scripture is of any private interpretation! With the laws of physics being what they are, I can't have this scripture yelled in an audible voice from the pages of this book, but if I could scream something, it would be this: No scripture is of any private interpretation and is not the will of men! We simply don't have what it takes to tell God His business. Who can be God's council (Romans 11:34)?

But, alas, it seems that this is what we do, and we have done it far too often, so we have arrived at forty-one thousand different churches. The simple Church that Jesus is the Christ, which began in Matthew and is solidified in Acts, has been fractured from one Rock into forty-one thousand different jagged pieces, with each being about how it is interpreted by the followers and less about what is said in God's Word. One group might believe the sprinkling of infants is baptism, whereas another group believes in total submersion of knowing adults, and instead of holding up scripture and saying that we will agree to follow what is written, it seems much easier to part ways, start another church, and agree to disagree—your group does it your way, and we will do it our way. Both sides are divided, and neither comes to an agreement with scripture while doing what seems right to them (Prov. 14:12; 16:25).

Humans are dividing the Church like broken pieces of pottery with jagged edges that cut and rip people and never form the beautiful mosaic God had intended. All because we add to, take from, and try to interpret God's Word.

These are the ground rules that must be followed: God's Word and nothing else. Whatever the topic, if it is not in the Bible, we cannot add it. And we must not take away from His word as to stop short of God explaining the Word to us in His detail.

Suppose Jesus simply said, "Blessed are those who mourn," and didn't finish the thought. I am sure we would walk around daily as long-faced, pouting creatures, looking for reasons to be sorrowful. When we allow Jesus to finish the thought, we see that we will be comforted and will walk in this light. We do not to add to this or take from it to see the true meaning.

If God were in charge of the Church, we would have ground rules, and it would be just God's Word—nothing more and nothing less.

Chapter 3

Just a Little Church History

Through my many and diverse years of following the Lord, I have had the opportunity to meet some wonderful people in service to the Master. One such person was a young, brilliant pastor of an old brick church. This wasn't just an old building; this was a church with history. It was well over two hundred years old and in a part of South Carolina that had seen Union and Confederate soldiers come through during bloody campaigns of the Civil War.

Axl Rose sang, "What's so civil about war anyway," and this church showed both the incivility of war and the civility of man because it was used as a hospital during the conflict and wasn't concerned about the color of your uniform. Blue and gray were secondary at the time to the red blood these men shed on the floors of this now old church.

Today, this church supports a hand-carved and polished placard explaining how they came to the rescue of soldiers during one of the most challenging times in the history of the United States. This placard, now appearing older itself, greets the churchgoers as they walk toward the building.

This aged, red brick building is nestled in trees that keep it cool during the hot South Carolina summers, and this is needed because the members of the church voted not install an updated air-conditioning unit in fear that the church may lose its antique luster. Someone mentioned to me that because the church was on the registry of the state, they could not change too many things about the church. Ceiling fans, however, were installed in the 1960s.

My friend, a young man in his thirties, was preaching to members of this historical and aristocratically church, whose fathers' fathers' grandfathers were charter members. He was a brilliant man with a heart and mind for God.

I visited him and this historically relevant church one Sunday morning, and the church service flowed from the opening two songs to the meet-and-greet, to the third song, to the offering, to a special song, and then to the service. The message was on Peter, as I remember correctly, and my friend didn't disappoint. His insight into the heart and mind of Peter was spot-on.

He spoke for about twenty minutes, and I could see his eye catch a glimpse of the clock hanging in the back of the sanctuary. In midsentence, midthought, and midscripture, my friend stopped and said, "Let's close in prayer." I wanted more! I wanted him to finish his sentence, his thought, and the scripture. Like a Saturday morning movie serial or a Batman television show, I was afraid I had to tune in next week to find out how it all ended.

Afterward, my friend met and greeted me, and I asked him why he didn't finish his thought. He said, "I have to get the people out of here at or before noon." The church deacons had voted that all sermons must end on time.

Over two hundred years of serving the community, walking on blood-stained floors, and being the home where church members have passed into the presence of God in the 1800s and 1900s, this is now a church of structure. A clock seems to rule the service. The Holy Spirit need only to be a spectator—and don't worry, we will get Him out on time too.

Church now seems scripted and timed more for convenience then efficiency.

I read this quote from John MacArthur and thought it was relevant.

> In our society, the definition of religion is very broad. Almost any belief system qualifies. But to God, any religion that doesn't produce holiness and sacrificial love is not true religion. That narrows the field considerably because anyone who isn't saved through faith in Jesus Christ remains in bondage to sin and has no capacity to live a holy and selfless life.

Pop Quiz: How long is the church era? Five thousand years? Two thousand years? Forever?

Church history begins in Matthew 16 and continues until Revelation 4. Church is first mentioned by Jesus in Matthew 16, and the Church is mentioned last in Revelation 3:14, when Jesus judges the seven groups of people in the Church. The church season is short, and as we will see, humans have taken it from one Church, that Jesus is the Christ, to forty-one thousand different churches. How could such a thing happen?

The problem, like all problems, is that humans take charge and get in the way of what God had planned. Adam got in the way of God's plan when he ate from the tree, just as the Pharisees and Sadducees got in the way of God's plan by putting so many rules and regulations on the people that they couldn't keep up. The Church path from Matthew to the second chapter of Acts, to the church today is a crooked way because we somehow think that

God Almighty needs our help, or the most common problem: I want my say-so. Either way, we forget to let God and His Word be in charge, and everything else will fall into place.

Humans are is in charge now. Churches of today now seem to revolve around humans, traditions, religion, and interpretations of what we think God wants. The church service is turned into either a religious exercise or an emotional free-for-all, with neither being what God intended His church to be.

I find myself guilty of it too because we have a consistent structure to our Sunday service. In our service, we sing two hymns, have opening announcements, and have another hymn. Then we pray, take up the offering, and sing one more hymn before a special song is given. Like clockwork, we go through these steps before the service. I am not like my friend, where I need to see what time it is to finish the service, but I do know that about eight pages of notes is about thirty minutes, and I do keep this in mind.

Even the close of the service is planned as we lead to an altar call that must be given. I remember preaching one Sunday morning to a local church that was dying. In the building, I had three people. An older woman who had grown up in this church was seventy-two, and she had lost her husband recently; when he was alive, they never missed a service in their fifty-five years of marriage. The other two people were a seventy-year-old woman and her fifty-two-year-old son. The son was the last remaining deacon of the church and was trying to keep the doors of that church open. At the close of the service, like all good Southern Baptist preachers, I began to give the invitation to receive Jesus as Lord and Savior to three people who have been attending this church for a combined 192 years. The invitation was given just like clockwork.

We seem to have abandoned the idea that the Church of Jesus Christ *is* Jesus Christ, and we have turned church into a series of gestures and timed activities, all in the name of good intentions and religion. From holy water to scripted calls to salvation, humans have taken the gospel of Jesus Christ and added their own "This is how you do it" to the faith. We have gone from worshiping our Lord to the religion of duty, from being the church to "doing church."

I think it would be accurate to say that when it comes to God, we have more good intentions than good works. As churchgoers, we mean well and want to help with good intentions and committed hearts. Even today, with our good intentions, we seem to feel that if we are all right with what we are doing, it is for God, and our hearts are in it, then it must be all right to do, whatever it is. From vows of poverty and celibacy to handling snakes and laughing in the name of God, humans try to determine what is in God's best interest.

These good intentions started out innocently early enough. The Church began to take shape in the book of Acts with camaraderie and unity. Since then, it has gone through having a government-run church in Rome, to a Crusades, to the Great Protestant Reformation and the Great Awakening, to the birth of the churches in America. If I were to ask my group of believers when the Southern Baptist movement started, I am sure most would say in the1600s, when people started inhabiting America. If I were to ask my friends in the Charismatic movement when their followings began, I am sure they would say in the second chapter of Acts.

The Southern Baptist started in 1845, and the Pentecostal movement began in 1906. I am more than willing to guess that neither follows the example of church given in Acts. I am not throwing stones; I am simply telling you that when humans get involved, we seem less likely to follow what God says. Why form a Southern Baptist Convention, Pentecostal movement, or Watch Tower Society? Why not sit down with other believers and see what God says about His church in His book? Why start another church or movement when there is only supposed to be one?

Humans moving through the Church is not a new issue that was created in 1845 or 1906. Men putting their two cents in began long ago. I am going to mention some of the things added to church throughout history, and I am not going to criticize. I am simply going to say that these things were added to church with good intentions, but I cannot find scriptural references for them, so I believe that they are added to scripture (see Deut. 4 and Rev. 22).

The Church was being persecuted heavily during the first couple centuries, and it began to get strength in Rome by merging with other non-Christian groups. Different things were being added to the Church in the name of unity and compromise, and although those things may have sounded logical at the time, I do not believe they were added to the church by God because God Himself would be in violation of Deuteronomy 4 and Revelation 22.

I got the following from the Gotquestions.org website.

> For the first 280 years of Christian history, Christianity was banned by the Roman Empire, and Christians were terribly persecuted. This changed after the "conversion" of the Roman Emperor Constantine. Constantine provided religious toleration with the Edict of Milan in AD 313, effectively lifting the ban on Christianity. Later, in AD 325, Constantine called the Council of Nicea in an attempt to unify Christianity. Constantine envisioned Christianity as a religion that could unite the Roman Empire, which at that time was beginning to fragment and divide. While this may have seemed to be a positive development for the Christian church, the results were anything but positive. Just as Constantine refused to fully

embrace the Christian faith, but continued many
of his pagan beliefs and practices, so the Christian
church that Constantine promoted was a mixture
of true Christianity and Roman paganism.

In an effort to unify Rome, Constantine tried a peaceful unity of
faiths by folding all the religions together. It kind of sounds like
our leaders trying to unify humans by telling Godly people to
accept not-so-Godly things today under the umbrella of tolerance.
However, since the unification in AD 313, we have added these
nonbiblical things to the Church.

> 431: Council of Ephesus determines that Mary can
> be worshiped as the mother of God.
> 500: Common priestly dress code must be
> adhered to.
> 565: Justinian regards "Church of State" ordained.
> 607: The title of pope is given.
> 786: Practice of worship of relics and images
> decreed.

In the first six hundred years of the Church, we accepted the
worship of someone other than Christ, went back to priestly
garb and phylacteries, accepted a type of one-world religion, and
appointed one *man* as the head of the church.

> 850: Holy water is instituted.
> 995: Canonization of dead saints begins.
> 998: Fasting on Fridays begins.
> 1070: Celibacy of priest is instituted.

Two hundred more years pass by, and we begin to think that by
men blessing water, it becomes holy, and that by lifting up men as
saints, this somehow gets the kingdom to grow. Fasting on Friday
and celibacy issues are works created by humans in the name of
good intentions, but they have no scriptural basis.

1084: Execution of nonconverts to Christianity begins.
1090: Prayer beads (rosary) is instituted.
1215: The belief in Transubstantiation begins.

I am sure this is where some will close this book and throw it away, but I encourage you to continue to read. These things I have listed and the years they were instituted are vital in showing that as humans, we have the best intentions of doing this in remembrance of God and our commitment to Him. What I am challenging is the validity of these things. I am trying to show you that they are not in the Bible, and we must be cautious of adding to His Word. The penalty is too great to ignore the warnings given in Revelation 22.

The next historical reference is in 1249, when the reading of the Bible by laymen is prohibited. From 1249 to the 1600s, the common man did not have a Bible and was not allowed to read a Bible. The major problem that arose from that was that humans must now trust other people for the truth. Acts 17:11 tells us to search the scriptures to find out if what we are hearing is true, but at this time in history, most people could not do that. A priest could stand up and say that the Holy Spirit was the color blue, and laymen had no choice but to believe the priest.

Instead of the Bible as being our source of all divine truth, people had to trust the priests to give them truth. Now, I don't want to hurt anyone's feelings, but aren't priests just men? And are not all men deceitful, liars, and wicked in nature? No offense, but don't tell me the Word—give me the Word.

1439: Purgatory decreed.
1492: Jesus outlawed in Spain.
1545: Church tradition deemed "equal authority to the Bible."
400–1600: Independent study of the Bible is outlawed.

In 1611, the King James Bible was written so common people could have God's Word at their fingertips. At this time, the Protestant Reformation was beginning to take shape, and I think it was safe to say there were two Christian churches at that time, the Protestants and the Catholics. Since then, forty-one thousand different versions have appeared. As if everyone who could read a Bible read things one's own way and, in rebellion or ignorance, thought that starting a church was being part of a franchise, like a McDonald's or Taco Bell. People seemed less focused on the truth that it is all about God, and they turned their focus to building bigger buildings and Sunday school attendance.

As churches began sprouting up like weeds, we find that when we are at a difficult passage or a spiritual crossroads, we make our own fork in the road, and one misunderstanding of scripture goes one way while another misunderstanding of scripture goes another.

Jack Van Impe is quoted as saying,

> The Laodicean era (in Revelation chapter 3) is a highly prosperous one. As a result, her people have erected elaborate church structures worth millions of dollars. (Stop for a moment and consider the money presently being invested in buildings used one to three hours weekly.) Laodicean pastors often attack the "electronic church" ministries. The command of Jesus is, "Go ye into all the world and preach the gospel to every creature (Mark 16:15). However, the "electronic church" ministers are simply obeying the Savior. God help each of us to see that although buildings are necessary for worship and service, they should be humble edifices rather than the latest multi-million dollar architectural monstrosities which glorify men.

The church isn't the next, newest, and coolest building being built. The church is not the oldest way to practice a church function. The church is that Jesus is the Christ, and this is what we are to follow.

We are warned by Jesus on two occasions to beware of false teachers (Matt. 7; Matt. 24), and we seem to ignore it. We seem to ignore Paul's warnings of false teachers (2 Tim. 4:3) and Jude's warnings (Jude 11), and we abandon sound teaching for beautiful buildings, church tradition, clever preachers, and programs, all the while seeking Godless direction.

All in the name of "church."

Chapter 4

Beware of False Prophets

I magine, if you can, that a well-known and popular travel agent has contacted you and said that there is an incredible deal for you to take your family to Disney World. All your friends know and use this travel agent, and when he tells you to pack your bags, take the next week off work, get your kids out of school, and start driving, you are glad to do it.

The agent tells you that the free tickets will be waiting for you at the gate, with Mickey and Minnie at Disney World. All you have to do is follow his directions and then enjoy Disney World.

He tells you that you must drive by his directions—not in a straight line, because there may be a detour or two you will need to take before you claim your prize. He tells you, "A straight path to the park would be what others might do, but you are different than others, and you need to embrace your uniqueness and take a different way." You put your faith in the agent, and you drive.

He tells you that you first need to drive down an unfamiliar road, which is brightly lit and exciting, for many miles while you listen to classic rock music on the radio. There are many, many cars on this exciting road, all following one another, and the classic rock music is good, so nothing seems out of place or odd. You keep driving. Besides, can all these other drivers be going in the wrong direction?

The travel agent then calls and tells you that there is a detour ahead, but it is a wonderful detour. He tells you not to worry or be alarmed and adds that there is a museum dedicated to the works of the Gummy Bear ahead, and it is something that you can't resist. You feel the detour is taking you in the opposite direction from the promised Disney World, but you can't resist, and you trust the travel agent, so you drive.

There is a fee to see the Gummy Bear attraction, but it seems reasonable, and after your fill of gummy bears, you turn to get back to the unfamiliar road and continue your drive to the theme park. You don't quite seem to get all the way back to the main road before your agent calls again and tells you of another magnificent event that you must see. You still fell you are heading in the wrong direction from your destination, and you feel that your time is running thin with the trip to enjoy Disney World, but you trust your agent; he should know your travel and time constraints. So you agree.

He tells you there is a parade a few cities away, and the grand marshal of the parade is Elmo from the Muppets, and everybody loves Elmo … So you drive. The city is not in the same direction as Disney World, but the agent, whom everybody knows and trusts, wouldn't mislead you. So you drive.

After a magnificent parade, where you posted a selfie with Elmo on Facebook, you get back on the road to Disney World. There is a worry in your car that the clock is ticking, and you are going to enjoy less time in the destination promised to you, but you trust your agents. Besides that, there is the additional worry that if you don't do things the way your travel agent wants you to do it, you may not be able to get your free tickets when you get there. So you drive.

Your cell phone rings again. It's the travel agent, and he says, "Get off at the next exit. There's something you need to see!"

You follow directions that you know are not straight to a destination without a ticket … You are being diverted by wonderful exciting adventures that have nothing to do with your promised goal but with bright lights, good music, celebrity, and sweets. Your final goal is an elusive vision of a promised future that was never really there in the first place.

So are the promises of false teachers.

If God were in charge of the Church, don't you think He would warn us of pitfalls and problems that can happen within the Church? One such problem that God would warn us of is false teachers who can come in if we let them. With forty-one thousand churches, there are plenty of false teachers to go around. Before we get off on the wrong foot concerning false teachers, it's time for a pop quiz.

Pop Quiz: What is a false teacher?

A false teacher is someone who teaches falsely. It is really no more complicated than that. We can sometimes get a picture in our minds of a person who stands up, denounces God and His Son, and rails against the things of God. Not so. A false teacher will speak of God, speak of Jesus, and speak of the Bible, but somewhere his message gets lost in falsehoods. God would warn us of such things if He were in charge of the church.

If you own a red letter edition Bible and see everything that Jesus said is printed in red ink, you can see Jesus said many, many things. He is the Son of God and is incapable of lying, and with that alone, we should believe everything He took the time to tell us.

Concerning the truth, Jesus said to Pilate, "For this cause I was born, and for this cause I have come into the world, that I should bear witness to the truth. Everyone who is of the truth hears My voice" (John 18:37). Jesus said that He came into the world to bear witness to the truth, and everything that He said and is will be the truth.

Jesus said that the greatest commandment is to love the Lord your God with all your heart, soul, and strength, and we believe Him. He told us to love thy neighbor as thyself, and we believe Him. He said He was going away to prepare a place for us, and we believe Him.

Speaking on the end-time, Jesus said this in Matthew 24:11, "And many false prophets shall rise, and shall deceive many." Deceived by false prophets? If we believe that everything Jesus has ever said was true, we must believe this. False prophets will rise, and many people will be deceived.

I can almost hear the critics now: "Not me! Not in my church! False teachers and prophets are not welcome in my church!" They feel as if by shutting the door and turning the lock, Satan and false teachers are kept out. Then where would they be? "Surely the many believers that will be deceived must mean those other churches, not the churches I don't go to … Those must be the one deceived, not me."

Pop Quiz: Who will be deceived?

People who do not follow Jesus or go to church will not be the ones being deceived. They are deceived already. It is the people who want to follow Jesus who will be deceived—churchgoers like you and me.

I want us to see something now. What is a prophet? A prophet is one who speaks for God, or should I say "his" god. Today, a prophet isn't one who tells the future. We know the future already (Revelation, Daniel, Joel, etc.).

When we see the word *prophesy* or *prophet* in the Bible, it is *nabiy* in the Old Testament Hebrew and *prophētēs* in the New Testament Greek. Here is the meaning of a prophet: "Men filled with the Spirit of God, who by God's authority and command in words of weight pleads the cause of God and urges salvation of men." Not seers of the future but spokespeople for God. Sounds like 2 Peter to me.

A prophet "pleads the cause of God," or his god. To prophesy is to profess the things of God. There were some times that a prophet spoke of future things. Daniel and the apostle John should come to mind, but that does not mean that Peter and Paul, or James, should not be included as those who are prophets of God. They speak for God, and that is to profess what God wants them to profess.

In the Old Testament, the books written are considered from major and minor prophets, but some speak of things to come, and some do not. For example, 1 Kings 18:22 says, "Then said Elijah unto the people, I, *even* I only, remain a prophet of the LORD; but Baal's prophets *are* four hundred and fifty men". Elijah is called a prophet, and so are the men of Baal. At this time, Elijah is not speaking on things to come in the future, but he is a spokesman for the Lord. Baal's men are called "the prophets for Baal," meaning that they speak for Baal, their god.

Today's prophet would profess God and His Word to a lost and fallen world. Today's prophet would profess what is truth: that all men are sinners that need a Savior. Today's prophet would profess that this is a current problem, not a future one. He would profess that there is a solution: Jesus Christ. He would profess this current solution (Jesus) to the current problem (sin). Today's prophet would profess that God currently loves the world and has

41

given His son to save humankind. He would not be prophesying this as a future vision but a current dilemma. This is no longer the future promise spoken of by Isaiah and the Psalmist, but a current truth as spoke by Peter and Paul.

Today's prophet will tell you about Jesus. A prophet today would not tell you another way other than Jesus. A prophet today would not tell you of new sins that need to be addressed. Today's prophet would profess that Jesus is the Christ—not will be the Christ, but is the Christ. Not a future picture, but a current solution.

In 1 Corinthians 14:24, Paul talks about an unbeliever coming into your assembly, and it says, "But if all prophesy, and an unbeliever or an uninformed person comes in, he is convinced by all, he is convicted by all." That is, he hears God being pleaded, and he then is convinced and convicted not by future prophecies but by what is currently spoken of God. It is the present trouble of sin that he is convicted of, not the future prophecy of it. To prophecy, speak prophesies, or be a prophet means to be God's spokesperson for the cause of Jesus Christ, not to see the future. The future is already written and planned out.

Today's prophet could not give a new message about Jesus Christ, and a prophet today could not tell you of a future event beyond what is written in the Bible.

Could today's prophet tell you of the coming judgment on the world that Daniel in his book, or John in Revelation, has missed? Could today's prophet tell you something about heaven that Paul, John, and the other writers of the Bible left out? Could God get to the point where He comes back to us two thousand years later and says, "Oops, I missed something"? If He did, and He is not done, we then need to open the Book of Mormon and the Koran and give them attention.

Because Revelation 22:18 warns us about adding to God's Word, we cannot have any "new" words from God. If people were to stand in a church today, on a stone in the square, or in an auditorium and say they are prophets sent from God with a "new" message, they would violate Revelation 22:18, which says, "If any man shall add unto these things, God shall add unto him the plagues that are written in this book." Through the Holy Spirit of God, John, in Revelation, is echoing what Moses said in Deuteronomy 4:2, "You shall not add to the word which I command you, nor take from it, that you may keep the commandments of the LORD your God which I command you."

Nothing can be added. There are no new prophecies. It is complete!

God hasn't missed anything. Some have reduced God to an old man who had people write a book years ago, and after two thousand years or so, He needs to revise it to bring it up to speed because humans think they are different. It is as if after two thousand years or so, God woke up and said, "Oh, by the way, I forgot something …" God doesn't need our help and has no revisions to make. We have not surprised God by all of the sudden being smarter than the last generation. God does not need to "update" His book because we now have faster cars, tweets, and high-speed internet service.

The current church establishments that most Protestants would challenge as cults believe that we have the power to change scripture. To add to what most consider the Bible, the Old and New Testament, Mormons have the Book of Mormon, Muslims have the Koran, and Jehovah's Witnesses have their own rendering of a rewritten Bible that supports their beliefs. If we as professing Protestants feel we can prophesy a new message today, we would be as guilty as they are, and we would be in violation of 2 Peter 1, Revelation 22, and Deuteronomy 4.

Let me give you an example of something that is a hot topic today. Lately, many books have been written about heaven. Many have been written about traveling to heaven and seeing heaven. The movie *Heaven Is Real* is about a small boy going to heaven and visiting Jesus Christ, God, and the Holy Spirit.

Pop Quiz: How could we know whether or not this trip was real?

The only way that we can say any message is from God is if it lines up with what is previously written in the Bible. All messages from God must line up with scripture, or they violate Deuteronomy 4:2 and Revelation 22:18–19, which tell us not to add or take away from the Word. Any word from or about God must be in the Bible. Please let me repeat that: All things pertaining to God must be in the Bible. It is the complete source of God and His direction that He lifts scripture above His very name.

Colton Burpo is the young boy who says he went to heaven and came back. Colton says many things about his trip, and here are a couple things: Colton says that he met Jesus, then he met the Holy Spirit, and then he met God Himself. When asked what the Holy Spirit looked like, Colton said that He had a blue color about Him. Colton said the Holy Spirit was blue. Colton went on to say that he was in heaven long enough to get his wings and his halo.

We need to ask ourselves a very simple question: Does the Bible say that the Holy Spirit is blue and that when we all get to heaven, believers will have wings and halos?

The following is from Eric Johnson's blog, Grace to You:

> Lynn Vincent, who ghost-wrote "Heaven is for Real" on behalf of the young boy Colton Burpo and his father, said that she was initially reluctant to include Colton's description of people in heaven having wings. "If I put that people in Heaven have wings, orthodox Christians are going to think that the book is a hoax." She did and they didn't.

Johnson goes on to say, "Evangelical readers' discernment skills are at an all-time low, and that is why books like these proliferate. Despite the high profile, high sales figures, and high dollar amounts Christian publishers can milk from a trend such as this, it doesn't bode well for the future of Christian publishing—or for the future of the evangelical movement."

This is a vivid and far too bright picture of not only false teachers but false disciples. Heaven does not teach that we will have wings and halos when we get to heaven. That is why the ghostwriter of the book said that true evangelicals will think the story is a lie. Why? Because it doesn't line up with scripture, and that is the only test.

We would like to excuse it away by saying because this was a little boy, he didn't really know what he saw. We would love to say that with every so-called heaven experience, the people didn't understand what they were seeing, so they tried to put into words things that cannot be explained. We would also like to excuse away things like this because, as Fox Mulder of *The X-Files* would say, we want to believe. The issue shouldn't be with what near-death people say they saw. The issues shouldn't be with what I want to believe. The issue is this: Is it what scripture said it should be? What does God in His Word say on this or any issue?

If the Bible says that angels have wings and humans do not, we trust the Bible, not a million personal experiences. The Bible tells us that when we get to heaven, there will be this: "Then I looked, and I heard the voice of many angels around the throne, the living creatures, and the elders; and the number of them was ten thousand times ten thousand, and thousands of thousands" (Rev. 5:11).

Angels, elders, and creatures all have their place in heaven, and nowhere are we told that we would have wings and halos. Jesus at His resurrection is an example of how we should be seen when we get to heaven. Because there was no talk of wings on Jesus when Mary talked to Him at the tomb, or when the couple talked to Him on the road to Emmaus, or when Peter, James, the five hundred, or Paul saw Him, and because there was no shock and awe about this man having wings and a halo and no mention was given of them, our resurrected bodies will not have them either.

Our faith cannot be the Bible plus what someone experienced, saw, felt, or opined.

The false disciples are the people who call themselves followers of Jesus Christ but who do not know scripture well enough to discern a false teaching from a true teaching. We are softened to believe falsely when we see paintings of men with halos, statues of men with wings, and other false religious depictions. Then when it comes to discernment, we believe what tradition, cute little boys, and society has produced over what God has said in His Word.

If Jesus Christ Himself tells us in Matthew 24:11, "And many false prophets shall rise, and shall deceive many," shouldn't we have the scriptural obligation to be on the lookout for them? There is a possibility that there are 40,999 false beliefs in the world, and each of us has to search the scriptures (Acts 17:11) to see the validity of our own faith.

A young lady visited our humble church, and during a conversation with her, she called her little Louisiana city "the speed trap capital of the world." That may be an exaggerated statement, however because of her warning, I know to slow down before I go through her city. I heard the warning of the speed trap, and I will act accordingly. I will look for it, and when I see it, I will respond in a mature and responsible manner.

I am a bivocational pastor who also delivers the mail, and once after a heavy rain, I saw a sign on the road that said, "Bridge is out." I didn't have to go any farther; I turned around and went out another way. I heeded the warnings given to me and responded in a mature and responsible manner.

Near the end of the Sermon on the Mount, Jesus issued this stark warning to His listeners: "Beware of the false prophets, who come to you in sheep's clothing, but inwardly are ravenous wolves" (Matt. 7:15).

We are told by Jesus to love the Lord our God with a whole heart, mind, soul, and strength; that He is the only way to the Father; that we should pay our taxes (give unto Caesar what is Caesars); and that our worship has to exceed that of the Pharisees and Sadducees. He also tells us to beware of the false prophets, and although we may listen to Him as an authority and expert in those other areas, I feel the church takes the false prophet warning as advice to be taken with a grain of salt.

False prophets were not new to Israel. As long as God has had true prophets, Satan has had false ones. They are seen from the earliest times of redemptive history. Moses warned,

> If a prophet or a dreamer of dreams arises among you and gives you a sign or a wonder, and the sign or the wonder comes true, concerning which he spoke to you, saying, "Let us go after other gods (whom you have not known) and let us serve them," you shall not listen to the words of that prophet or that dreamer of dreams; for the Lord your God is testing you to find out if you love the Lord your God with all your heart and with all your soul. You shall follow the Lord your God and fear Him; and you shall keep His commandments, listen to His voice, serve Him, and cling to Him. But that prophet or that dreamer of dreams shall be put to death, because he has counseled rebellion against the Lord your God. (Deut. 13:1–5)

Did you see that? God is testing you to see if you keep His commands and listen to His voice. Where do we do that? The Bible!

The false prophet is put to death. This is not an issue that God takes lightly. Moses tells the people to discern on the side of God, not the false prophet. Moses says those who do not fear the Lord, keep His commandments (His Word), listen to His voice (His Word), serve Him, and cling to Him are considered rebels against God and should be put to death. If we kept that standard today, we would have fewer charlatans in the pulpits taking advantage of well-meaning people who trust their leaders. I know of no man or woman who feels that he or she is following the blind leaders, but far too many are, and if they don't open our eyes through the truth of scripture, all will end up in the ditch.

Elsewhere in the Old Testament, God told the prophet Jeremiah, "The prophets are prophesying falsehood in My name. I have neither sent them nor commanded them nor spoken to them; they are prophesying to you a false vision, divination, futility and the deception of their own minds" (Jer. 14:14). It never ceases to amaze me that if we are given the location of a speed trap or a bridge is out, we listen. We listen to those present-day driving warnings and take actions. However, it seems that with all these warnings about false teachers, we keep driving at break-neck speeds, heading directly toward the dangerous bridge that is out.

Did the phrase by Jeremiah, "prophesying falsehood in My name," catch your attention? False prophets speaking in the name of God misleading people–this sounds exactly like the statement Jesus made in Matthew 7:22, "Many will say to Me in that day, 'Lord, Lord, have we not prophesied in Your name, cast out demons in Your name, and done many wonders in Your name?'" Many will say, "Didn't we prophecy in Your name?" Please get this: many will speak in the name of Jesus! Many false prophets will preach, pray for healing, and "do wonders," all in the name of Jesus. Are you doing things in the name of Jesus that are not in the Bible? That started in the Old Testament and is rampant in churches today.

Paul warned the Roman believers, "Now I urge you, brethren, keep your eye on those who cause dissensions and hindrances contrary to the teaching which you learned, and turn away from them. For such men are slaves, not of our Lord Christ but of their own appetites; and by their smooth and flattering speech they deceive the hearts of the unsuspecting" (Rom. 16:17–18).

I can't help but think of these charlatans on television who constantly seem to have their hands out asking for money. I have heard television preachers tell their listeners to send them their tithe money—not to take it to the church they attend but mail it to the television preachers. I have heard some ask their audience to make them executive of their estates after they have died.

I remember Jim Baker taking millions from unsuspecting, God-loving followers in the name of Jesus to feed his own personal appetites. These are false prophets in sheep's clothing who are ravenous wolfs devouring all they can. There is a church not too far from my house that makes an estimated $63 million a year, and I have tried to see whether they support a missionary or have an outreach to the poor or sister building to reach the lost. My research has come up empty. "Lord, Lord ... Did we not make millions in Your name?"

My wife asked me if I was uncomfortable mentioning names in the pulpit of those who I feel are false teachers. No, I am not uncomfortable with it. A problem arises when you do mention names, and the problem is this: people would rather follow men than be subject to learning and obeying scripture. If I were to point out the flaws in Joseph Smith to a Mormon, the Mormon follower would much rather dismiss scripture than dismiss Joseph Smith. I am sure earlier in the book, the first time I mentioned I was a Baptist preacher, some people put down the book and had enough.

Today, we as believers we would rather "stand by your man," as Tammy Wynette said in the old country song, than put words and actions to the test of scripture. Should we name names? John the Baptist did! Matthew 3:17 states, "But when he saw many of the Pharisees and Sadducees coming to his baptism, he said to them, 'Brood of vipers! Who warned you to flee from the wrath to come?'" I can hear the people of today say, "John! Be careful! I know those Pharisees, and I know those Sadducees, and I follow them on the radio. My preacher mentions their names a lot, so don't you call them names, like a brood of vipers! Who are you to judge?"

Some would argue, "Well, He didn't mention names, just groups." How about from Paul? First Timothy 1:18–19 says, "Concerning the faith have suffered shipwreck of whom are Hymenaeus and Alexander, whom I delivered to Satan that they may learn not to blaspheme." Paul named names not only for Timothy to be aware of them but also to allow Hymenaeus and Alexander to learn a lesson. Paul didn't caudle them and keep them around. He didn't worry about Sunday school count or one fewer tithe check in the plate. He named names for everybody's well-being.

Not to have you think it is just a Paulian thing, the apostle John says in 3 John 1:9–10, "I wrote something to the church; but Diotrephes, who loves to be first among them, does not accept what we say. For this reason, if I come, I will call attention to his deeds which he does, unjustly accusing us with wicked words; and not satisfied with this, he himself." Do you know any church leaders who love to be first, lifted up among the people? Do you know those who love to cause problems in the church with lies and falsehoods? John pointed him out and said, "See him over there? Yeah, him! Diotrephes! Keep your distance from him!"

Even Jesus, our Lord and Savior who so loved the world that He died for us; pointed out false teachers, referring to the Scribes, Pharisees, and Sadducees (very religious churchgoers); and called them hypocrites (Matt. 15), whitewashed tombs (Matt. 23), and liars (John 8). Matthew 23:27 reads, "Woe to you, scribes and Pharisees, hypocrites! For you are like whitewashed tombs which indeed appear beautiful outwardly, but inside are full of dead *men's* bones and all uncleanness." By today's standards, Jesus would have been called out for naming the Scribes and Pharisees. They must be pointed out just as a "Bridge is out" sign needs to be read. How else can we protect each other?

Pop Quiz: Whom do you blame? The wolves? Or the followers who are given every warning to follow but choose not to?

In other parts of the New Testament, false prophets are spoken of as "deceitful spirits" who advocate "doctrines of demons" (1 Tim. 4:1) and as those "who will secretly introduce destructive heresies, even denying the Master who bought them" (2 Pet. 2:1). People may say, "Well, truly those scriptures don't mean the people I follow, do they?"

What is a destructive heresy? Anything that is not from God. These people are in the forty-one thousand different denominations that we call church—destructive heresies secretly "brought in" to the churches. Secretly. None of these false teachers will parade the fact that they are teaching falsely. Most don't even realize it.

Here is what I believe is the first red flag as to who may be a false teacher: A great many of today's teachers would tell you that God wants the best for you, wants you to prosper and be in good health, and wants you to be happy. When the focus of the message give is on you and not Jesus Christ, it is time for you to yell, "Time out!"

Would you believe that my success isn't God's primary concern? My marriage, finances, health, and happiness will all end one day. What lives forever? Jesus Christ and His kingdom. That is God's primary focus and concern. My wallet means very little to God. It means very little to Him when I try to fill it to support a religious cause, and it means very little to Him when I try to fill it to support myself. My church attendance, Sunday school attendance, tithe check, incense, laughing, and falling in church mean little to God. The only thing that matter is Jesus Christ and what I have done with Him. If I were to imagine that my happiness and success was the prime concern of Jesus, I think He would have to rewrite Matthew 5, the beatitudes.

Those warnings are summarized in the word translated *beware* in Matthew 7:15, "Beware of false prophets, who come to you in sheep's clothing, but inwardly they are ravenous wolves." It is not a call simply to notice or sense something, but to be on guard against it because it is so harmful. The word conveys the idea of holding the mind away.

John MacArthur is quoted as saying,

> False prophets are more than wrong; they are dangerous, and we should not expose our minds to them. They pervert thinking and poison the soul. False prophets are spiritual beasts and are immeasurably more deadly than the physical ones. Both Peter and Jude call them "unreasoning animals" (2 Pet. 2:12; cf. Jude 10).

Ravenous wolves … Unreasonable animals … Speed trap! Bridge is out! Be on alert!

Paul calls them "savage wolves." Paul's last words to the Ephesian elders, when he met with them for a farewell on the beach near Miletus, included a somber warning about inevitable false teachers. "I know that after my departure savage wolves will come in among you, not sparing the flock; and from among your own selves men will arise, speaking perverse things, to draw away the disciples after them. Therefore be on the alert" (Acts 20:29–31).

Savage wolves will come in among us, not sparing the flock. They come from among our own selves to draw away disciples after them.

Therefore, be on alert.

Chapter 5

Apostates

A friend of mine and I were having a great discussion concerning the use of spiritual gifts in churches today. I am very excited that we took the time to open the Bible and see what God says on these issues. Far too many times, we argue different points of view, debating what I think as opposed to what you think, and we fall short to see what God says on issues.

Just before we took our powerful religious stance to "agree to disagree," my friend said she was going to send me an email she received. The email was on "Laughing in the Spirit." I love writing and try to pay attention to how something is written, especially how something begins. Whenever I receive anything that starts, "You are not going to believe this," I generally don't believe it. The email about laughing in the Spirit from my friend began with the statement "Another thing under attack is …" and went into a treatise defending the stance of laughing in the Spirit.

"Agree to disagree" is being replaced by "Under attack" as the newest catchphrase in church belief. We no longer agree to disagree—I now believe that you are attacking me. It appears that there is no longer a need to talk about the issues, to disagree or come to an agreement. Now, when you voice an opinion, voice your belief, or open the Word, and I don't agree with you, you are attacking me. Honest and open investigation and debate with the Bible uncovered now are thrown out the window.

Jude 1:4 says, "For certain men have crept in unnoticed," and while that may have been true two thousand years ago, certain men have now bullied their way into the church, yelling, "Don't attack my false teachings!" Grown men are allowed to bring their heresy into the church, and the political correctness of the day leads the way because we cannot question the heresy without being accused of attacking someone.

The email I received having the first line voicing the stance of attack had the second line saying of the writer, "In my opinion …" The writer says "in my opinion" no fewer than four times. I don't want to hurt anyone's feeling, but I have to say when it comes to scripture, divine truth, or issues of spirituality, humans' opinions don't matter. When it comes to God, the only thing that matters is what He has written. Your opinion, my opinion, or the opinions of atheists do not matter and should carry no weight.

The writer of "Laughing" goes on to offer no scriptural basis for belief in this matter of a spiritual experience. As a matter of fact, the writer actually gives scriptural evidence *against* their stance as to this not being scriptural and not in the Bible in any way. However, the writer rested on one thing and confirmed, "I know how I feel when I do it."

With a fear of attacking this person, and their defenses already up, I am not allowed to get to the point where I can quote Proverbs 3:5, to "lean not on your own understanding." What a hater I would be if I pointed out that you cannot rest on how you feel. And what type of angry combatant would I become by pointing out that Jeremiah says we are deceitful and wicked, and Paul says we are liars and not to trust what comes out of a wicked, deceitful liar, so we can't rely on how I feel. I would be an attacking hater beating up people by pointing out scripture.

I would be tearing this person to shreds if I were to mention 1 Corinthians 12:7 and state that "the manifestation of the Spirit is given to each one for the profit of all." I was wondering how I personally profited by them giggling like schoolchildren at recess. Who got saved from this laughing? If I quote scripture and want to open the Bible with them, they yell, "Attacker!" and no open investigation or discussion is held or heard.

A man's opinion or feelings can never be the test as to what is from God. It seems that "my opinion," "your opinion," "my religion," and "my church" has become the litmus as to what God wants. So it is with apostates and those who want to change the truth of God to feelings, fables, and folly.

Another warning God would give to the Church if He were in charge would be to be on the lookout for apostates. An apostate is a close cousin to a false teacher, but the difference is that an apostate changes the truth for his own purposes. He abandons the truth. God would warn us of those who want to change the truth even the slightest bit. I heard it said that Satan doesn't mind if you are on target; he simply doesn't want you to hit the bull's-eye. Satan doesn't mind churchgoers or church; that is where he does his best work.

When I read through Jude, I was perplexed as to how a one-page "book'" with only twenty-five verses could be so long and not such an easy read. This small book in God's Word is complex and deep, and like most every book in the Bible, if read through too quickly, readers will let pass by more than they take in.

Jude's focus in verse four is on "certain men have crept in unnoticed" to the church, and the letter is on apostasy. What is apostasy? *Merriam-Webster's Dictionary* describes apostasy as "renunciation of a religious faith, abandonment of a previous loyalty."

Apostasy is an abandonment of a loyalty. When I was growing up, I thought an apostate was a person who stopped going to church or stopped believing and fell away. That is not always the case.

Apostasy is very much alive in churches and denomination all over the world. As a matter of fact, there just may be an apostate sitting right next to you in church. There may even be, God forbid, an apostate eating breakfast in your home. There might be an apostate brushing his or her teeth in your mirror in the morning.

An apostate is one who renounces a faith and abandons what he or she was once loyal to, and that can happen without leaving a church or changing denominations. Apostasy is abandoning what was once thought of as truth.

Pop Quiz: What is truth?

In our present time, truth is relative. By that I mean what is truth to you may not be truth to me. That is the credo of the world.

Friedrich Nietzsche said, "You have your way. I have my way. As for the right way, the correct way, and the only way, it does not exist." To Nietzsche and most of the world, truth does not exist. If I believe with all my heart and soul that Ford makes the best truck, and I believe that this is the truth, the whole truth, and nothing but the truth so help me God, all I have to do is bump into a Chevy man, and then my truth becomes mere opinion.

Concerning truth, Henry David Thoreau said, "Truths and roses both have thorns about them," leaving us to believe that a truth, though sweet smelling, can have painful results. I guess there is plenty of truth in that statement alone. Sometimes the truth hurts. It hurt Cain, Balaam, and Korah.

Jude 1:11 says this concerning apostates: "Woe to them! For they have gone in the way of Cain, have run greedily in the error of Balaam for profit, and perished in the rebellion of Korah." Jude mentions three men from the Old Testament in Cain, Balaam, and Korah, and he points out how they were apostates, those who abandoned truth for another way—their own way.

Cain should be a recognizable name, and if I were to mention his name and ask a common church attendee about Cain, I am sure I would get the answer that he was the one who murdered his brother Abel. Although that would be true, that is not why Jude brings his name up in verse 11. Cain was a murderer, but that was not his crime … at first.

> And in the process of time it came to pass that Cain brought an offering of the fruit of the ground to the LORD. Abel also brought of the firstborn of his flock and of their fat. And the LORD respected Abel and his offering, but He did not respect Cain and his offering. And Cain was very angry, and his countenance fell. (Gen. 4:3–5)

Abel brought an animal to sacrifice; Cain brought fruit.

I have heard many people come to Cain's defense: he was a farmer and brought what he could, and God should have looked at his heart and understood what Cain was trying to do. If we are looking for the truth here—and I think we should—the truth is that God said that there was a way to bring a sacrifice to Him, and all other ways were wrong. Period!

Cain tried to redefine truth. God said, "Here is truth. Sacrifice an animal!" I can't help but feel that Cain brought God a short list of reasons did not bring an animal. "God, can't you see that I am a farmer? My fruit is all I have. I don't have an animal to bring. I don't have the money to buy one. I'm not my brother, and I can't do it his way. I have only the best intentions. Surely you know my heart is in the right place." All those things may be true to Cain, but they do not change the truth that God Almighty has established. My personal reasoning doesn't circumvent God's truth. In this case, blood has to be shed as the only acceptable sacrifice. Fruit doesn't do that, and all the right excuses known to humankind don't change it.

Muhammed Ali said, "Rivers, ponds, lakes and streams—they all have different names, but they all contain water. Just as religions do—they all contain truths." We might agree with this quote, but we cannot let God's truth become something that is subjective to what I think His truth is. Cain (a churchgoer) was coming to the Lord and was also bringing his sacrifice to Almighty God, and there is truth in that. All religions may have truth in them, but Jesus is the Truth, and what He says goes without question from us.

Earlier, I quoted a saying from James McDonald: "Satan doesn't mind when you are on target … He just doesn't want you to hit the bull's eye." There is so much truth to that small statement. Cain knew God, talked to God, worshipped God, and brought a sacrifice to God. He was in the target but missed the mark because Cain did things Cain's way. An apostate changes the truth and misses the target.

Jude mentions Balaam, and his story is found in Numbers 22. The Israelites had camped too close to the Moabites, and these enemies of Israel's sent a contingency to speak to Balaam about getting them out of the area. "So the elders of Moab and the elders of Midian departed with the diviner's fee in their hand, and they came to Balaam and spoke to him the words of Balak" (Num. 22:7).

Don't read this too quickly! The Moabites came as spokesmen of Balak coming to talk to Balaam, God's prophet, with "the diviner's fee" to hire Balaam to curse his own people. Jude points out that Balaam's apostasy error was for profit.

When the Moabites came, Balaam talked to them and heard their message. He then talked to God about it. I wondered for a long time why Balaam even went to God with this issue. The Moabites came to a prophet of Israel and asked that prophet to curse his own people to get them out of the land. The answer right away should have been "No!" But when the people of Balak asked whether Balaam the prophet could curse them, it is as if Balaam looked at the money in the purse and said to the Moabite council, "Could I get back to you on that?" Then went to talk to God.

I can't help but feel that, like a good fisherman, the Moabites dangled the diviner's fee money before Balaam like bait to catch an unsuspecting fish. Balaam took it hook, line, and sinker.

When he talked to God, God tried to get Balaam to see what was going on. "Then God came to Balaam and said, 'Who are these men with you?'" (Num. 22:9). Of course God knew the answer. God knew who these people were. I think he was trying to get Balaam to see them for who they were and what they were doing there. It was as if God was asking Balaam, "Do you know who these people are? Come on, Balaam! Don't you know why they are here?" But Balaam couldn't see the Moabites or why they were there. All he could see were the dollar signs.

Blinded by the money waved in his face, Balaam still brought the issue to God. I could ask how many times we do that. We know what our first response should be to an issue, that being God's truth. But for some reason, we feel that either God will change His mind on what He was written, or He will at least understand why we are coming to Him on an issue that He has already decided long ago.

We do that, don't we? In our little local church, we know that God tells us not to gossip, but we find ourselves under the umbrella of "sharing our hearts" and "concern about Emma and her issues," so we talk about her, and after gossiping, we close in prayer. It is as if because we are Christians who love Emma and go to church with her, God will allow and even bless this gossip, because we feel it is important to us. We know better than that, don't we?

Balaam knew better. His first response should have been to tell the Moabites, "Don't let the door hit you on the back on your way out" but he didn't. He took it to God anyway, and after trying to get Balaam to see who he was dealing with in the Moabites, God didn't beat around the bush this time. "And God said to Balaam, 'You shall not go with them; you shall not curse the people, for they are blessed'" (Num. 22:12). God got right to the point. Don't go with them, and don't curse them, and that is the truth. Why Balaam had to hear what he already knew is the question. Why did Balaam go to God and hope He would understand? Because Balaam had another interest other than God's truth. There was the money, and the money seemed to speak louder than God's truth.

Numbers 22:21–22 states, "So Balaam rose in the morning, saddled his donkey, and went with the princes of Moab. Then God's anger was aroused because he went." Beloved, let this be a lesson to us all. God will never make you do the right thing. Balaam knew the right thing to do before he asked God. Balaam knew the right thing to do after he went to God, and Balaam knew the right thing to do when he went with the Moabites. It doesn't matter how many times we go to God as if we could get Him to understand our point of view. The bottom line? If you want to sin, if you want to do what God has said not to do, He is not going to stop you. He allows the pig to return to his slop and the dog to return to his vomit.

Balaam was asked to curse the people of Israel for money, and Balaam knew that God had blessed Israel and would never curse them. God said the people of Israel were blessed, and Balaam asked, "Could you curse them just this once? There is a lot of money riding on this." Balaam saw God's truth a different way because he looked through the eyes of money, not truth.

Here is the story of Korah and why he makes it to Jude's list.

> Now Korah the son of Izhar, the son of Kohath, the son of Levi, with Dathan and Abiram the sons of Eliab, and On the son of Peleth, sons of Reuben, took *men*; and they rose up before Moses with some of the children of Israel, two hundred and fifty leaders of the congregation, representatives of the congregation, men of renown. They gathered together against Moses and Aaron, and said to them, "*You take* too much upon yourselves, for all the congregation *is* holy, every one of them, and the LORD *is* among them. Why then do you exalt yourselves above the assembly of the LORD?" (Num. 16:1–3)

Korah led a revolt with "men of renown" against Moses and Aaron, questioning not only the leadership if Moses but also the fact that the God of Israel had even put them in charge. The impression was that Korah stirred up the people in Israel and got them to see things through his eyes. Sure, walking around the desert for years and eating the same food day after day may be a reason to complain for you and me, but Korah encouraged people to rise up against whom God had put in control. God put Moses in charge, and that was the truth that Korah tried to change.

Didn't Moses challenge Pharaoh? Didn't Moses usher in the plagues? Didn't Moses lead them to freedom out of Egypt? Didn't Moses part the sea? Didn't Moses find water in a rock? Didn't Moses ask for food, and it rained manna? Now, it would appear to Korah that Moses wasn't the instrument God should be using anymore.

When Moses went to God and talked to Him, God provided everything that Israel needed to head toward the Land of Milk and Honey. When we talk to God, through His Word He provides all we need to survive not only this life but also the life to come. Far too often we become like Korah, and when things don't go the way we think it should go, we want to dethrone God and put ourselves in charge.

The examples that Jude puts before us are common challenges to the church to this day—even more so now than they were in Genesis, Numbers, and Jude. The issues have not changed in five thousand, two thousand, or one hundred years. Humans still believe that they can bring an offering they want to before God with excuses why they didn't bring what He asked for. People still chase the not-so-almighty dollar in the name of God, and they still question the direction God would have them go.

Pop Quiz: Were Cain, Balaam, and Korah bad men?

I would be remiss if I didn't point out the fact that all three of these men were churchgoers. All three of these men thought that they were honoring God. Cain was bringing his sacrifice to God Almighty. Balaam was a spokesman for the God of Israel, so much so that the Moabites knew who to speak to concerning Israel. Korah, a priest, sis speak up for what he though was the concerns of all of Israel when he challenged Moses.

These men were not heathens who railed against God with damning heresies. All three of these men began their walks in the footsteps that God set before them. Cain brought his offering to God, Balaam brought his prayers to God, and Korah spoke up for what he thought God wanted. All three started out on the right path of truth and then walked a different way. All three continued on their crooked paths until God stepped in and had the final word.

About Cain, God said this: "A fugitive and a vagabond you shall be on the earth" (Gen. 4:12). After the improper offering that led to the jealous murder of his brother, God cast Cain out. "And Cain said to the LORD, 'My punishment is greater than I can bear!'" (Gen. 4:13). All Cain has known up to this point was his family and his God, and now he was without both. Being away from God should be more than any of us could bear.

Balaam didn't end well either. Balaam still collaborated with the Moabites, and then Numbers 31:8 records, "And they [the Israelites] slew the kings of Midian, beside the rest of them that were slain; namely, Evi, and Rekem, and Zur, and Hur, and Reba, five kings of Midian: Balaam also the son of Beor they slew with the sword." Balaam was killed away from the Israelites that he was raised in, that he was a spokesman for, that he was a prophet for, and that he prayed to God for. Like Cain, he died away from his place in God.

Could Balaam's death be any worse than Korah's? Numbers 16:32 says, "And the earth opened its mouth and swallowed them up, with their households and all the men with Korah, with all their goods." Korah, the men, their household, wives, children—everything was eaten alive. I can almost hear Korah singing out the old Frank Sinatra song "I Did It My Way" all the way to the bottom of the pit.

All three men died away from God and His blessing because all three men saw things a different way than God had told them. God had given them, as He does all of us, direction through His truth. Then humans (us included) somehow feel that they can question it and change it. We have bought in to this lie from Genesis, past Revelation, and into the church today.

Friedrich Nietzsche seems to be a spokesman for men when he said, "All things are subject to interpretation whichever interpretation prevails at a given time is a function of power and not truth."

We seem to see the truth of God as to what it means to me, instead of what God says to us. Cain thought a sacrifice was less than what God said it was, Balaam thought God wasn't serious about blessing Israel, and Korah thought he would be a better leader than one chosen by Almighty God. They simply relied on their own interpretations at a given time instead of God's truth.

John 18:38 records, "Pilate said to Him, 'What is truth?'" It is either divine direction or man's opinion. We cannot have it both ways. Apostasy abounds when we have God's Word and we say, "I know what it says, but I think it means …" with the words of Paul in Romans 1:21 echoing in our minds: "Because that, when they knew God, they glorified him not as God, neither were thankful; but became vain in their imaginations, and their foolish heart was darkened." We should protect ourselves from ourselves by being on alert from our vain imaginations and foolish hearts. The Word is enough and doesn't need to be helped along by doing it our way.

> There are joys which long to be ours. God sends ten thousands truths, which come about us like birds seeking inlet; but we are shut up to them, and so they bring us nothing, but sit and sing awhile upon the roof, and then fly away.
> —Henry Ward Beecher

> Jesus said to him, "I am the way, the truth, and the life. No one comes to the Father except through Me. (John 14:6)

Chapter 6

God's Apology Tour

W hen I was younger, I managed a Waffle House restaurant in North Carolina and found it very educational. When I applied for the job, I remembered all the times I visited a Waffle House, and it didn't seem to me that there was any difference from one store to the other. At the time, I took this for granted.

When Waffle House employees take your order, they yell the order to the cook in a coded message. "One order over with potatoes chunked, covered, and diced." The cook knows exactly what the person is talking about. Not only are you going to get good food, but there is a floor show that entertained.

Once the meal arrives, the plates are each displayed just as the pictures in the menu show them, and it doesn't seem to matter which Waffle House you go in, because each order is yelled out the same, and each plate is displayed the same appetizing way.

When I was going through my manager training, I asked if we could deviate from the ways things are supposed to be in the name of individual service, and my request was met with a resounding no. My trainer informed me that there was only one way to take an order at Waffle House and only one way to give an order at Waffle House. There was only one way to cook a meal at Waffle House, and there was only one way to display the meal at Waffle House.

If I were to change things up at Waffle House, even if I had the best intentions of the customer in mind, I would change what Waffle House is. This was a message that I received loud and clear. Waffle House does things the Waffle House way, and they are successful at it.

I can't help but think if the church took the advice of Waffle House, we might be in a different predicament. If we thought that there was only one way to worship and only one way to follow and one way to display ourselves, I don't think there would be forty-one thousand different ways to attempted success.

So far, we have set ground rules, looked at false teachers and apostates, and questioned why there are forty-one thousand different followings of Jesus Christ. I think now would be a good time to ask, "Is the Word of God still active, right, and just today? Jesus is the Word made flesh, and are He and the Word indeed the same yesterday, today, and forever? Did God change His mind about written revelation one hundred years ago, or one thousand years ago?"

I fully believe with my whole heart that Jesus is going to return on a cloud (Deut. 33; Ps. 68, 104; Dan. 7; Matt. 24, 26; Mark 13, 14; 1 Thess. 4; Acts 1; Rev. 1, 14), with all eyes beholding Him in such a glorious manner to bring His Church home with Him (1 Thess. 4:16). Then we will be with Him forever (John 14). I believe that with all my heart, soul, strength, and mind.

However, the way the Church of Jesus Christ is today, some would say God and His Word are old and antiquated, and the Bible needs revision and updating to meet a more modern world. Some deny the rapture of the Saints, and if that is the case, our Lord wouldn't come in glory. He would come for an apology tour instead. When Jesus returns, some see Him coming in humility to apologize to all those He misled and judged before our world became more tolerant to sin.

His first stop will be to be to apologize to Sodom and Gomorrah because He has already wiped them out in judgment. If we allow these same things in His Church today, He owes Sodom and Gomorrah a huge apology.

I received this bit of information from the website Human Rights Campaign:

> For example, the United Church of Christ ran a national television commercial that showed same-sex couples being welcomed into its congregations. The Presbyterian Church (USA) blesses same-sex unions. The Episcopal Church has issued an apology for past discrimination. And Reform Judaism ordains openly lesbian, gay and bisexual people as clergy.

Before you go there, no, I am not a homophobe or hater, and I am not addressing how the world does its thing. There should be no need for me to talk about how the world operates or tries to think with political correctness. And I am not addressing churches that open their doors to gay and lesbians for them to hear the message. I am addressing the men and women who change the Word of God to meet the standards of the world, and the churches that allow any leaders into their ranks who clearly defy what God says in His Word.

"And they called to Lot and said to him, "Where are the men who came to you tonight? Bring them out to us that we may know them carnally" (Gen. 19:5). This is why God destroyed Sodom and Gomorrah. It wasn't because they were rude and inhospitable guests. It was because of flagrant disregard of God's standard, and homosexuality was a huge part of it.

Leviticus 18:22 says, "You shall not lie with a male as with a woman. It is an abomination." Before you cry foul that this is an Old Testament passage and no longer valid, Paul says in Romans 1:27, "Likewise also the men, leaving the natural use of the woman, burned in their lust for one another, men with men committing what is shameful."

Has God changed His mind, and now all of a sudden, as if we could handle this now, He somehow is allowing this in the Church today? Are we to assume that God was dogmatic enough to call this an "abomination" and a "shameful" act years ago, but now we have cell phones, hundred-story buildings, and Starbucks, so God shouldn't be too upset anymore?

The glorious second coming of Christ has been replaced with the *Jesus Apology Tour,* and the bus would start here first. He would have to apologize to Sodom and Gomorrah for destroying them and then today allowing His leaders to do it. Then He would have to apology to Moses and Paul for making them look like liars for writing those passages.

It seems to me that it is as if, after a few years, people believe God can say, "Oh, yeah, never mind about that stuff, Moses and Paul. My bad, sorry. Changed My mind." Not so. If God said it to Moses, and Paul picked up the torch, no rainbow in the world is colorful enough to change God's Word. Indeed, Jesus, the Word, is the same yesterday, today, and forever.

Christians do not hate homosexuals, by the way, and God didn't intend for this to be a hate issue. The issue is obedience, and it has been clear since Adam and Eve that man has a problem with obedience. Man would rather disobey the God of creation to satisfy his own flesh than "resist the devil" (James 4:7) and follow Jesus Christ. When people crumble under the pressure because they want a fuller church or political gain, but some will not buy the products they're peddling, people fold up like cheap canvas tents on a windy day. The truth is that these politician haven't bought a vote—they have sold out God.

On the topic of obedience, Oswald Chambers said, "True liberty is the ability earned by practice to do the right thing." Following the words of Almighty God is the only thing that will ever bring us true liberty in this life.

I could imagine that if Jesus indeed came to apologize, the countless men and women who would support Him. Gay and lesbian activist groups, politicians, Muslims, and all other religious groups who claim another way other than Jesus. Billionaires would all donate to the cause. A colorful bus would be purchased. Maybe a jet plane with a painted fuselage that reads, "Just Kidding Tour 2020." The world would clamor for and support a movement like this.

Next stop on the apology tour: Achan, Ananias, Sapphira, and Simon the Sorcerer.

The story of Achan is found in Joshua 7 and involves a battle the Israelites were in. We are told in Joshua 7:1, "But the children of Israel committed a trespass regarding the accursed things, for Achan the son of Carmi, the son of Zabdi, the son of Zerah, of the tribe of Judah, took of the accursed things; so the anger of the LORD burned against the children of Israel." Achan took a spoil of war and hid it in his tent when God told them not to take anything from the battle. I am sure Achan must have thought that taking just a little bit for himself wouldn't matter much. Israel lost the battle because of the greed of just one man.

Joshua 7:19 states, "Now Joshua said to Achan, 'My son, I beg you, give glory to the LORD God of Israel, and make confession to Him, and tell me now what you have done; do not hide it from me.'"

In Joshua 7:21, Achan replied, "When I saw among the spoils a beautiful Babylonian garment, two hundred shekels of silver, and a wedge of gold weighing fifty shekels, I coveted them and took them. And there they are, hidden in the earth in the midst of my tent, with the silver under it."

What was God's response to Achan?

> Then Joshua, and all Israel with him, took Achan the son of Zerah, the silver, the garment, the wedge of gold, his sons, his daughters, his oxen, his donkeys, his sheep, his tent, and all that he had, and they brought them to the Valley of Achor. And Joshua said, "Why have you troubled us? The LORD will trouble you this day." So all Israel stoned him with stones; and they burned them with fire after they had stoned them with stones. (Josh. 7:24–25)

Achan, all that he had stolen, all his property, his sons and his daughters, killed and burned. Those who think they can use God today for the sole reason of turning a buck should heed this warning. Does God now have to apologize to Achan and his family?

The story of Ananias, with Sapphira, is well-known. Acts 5 details how they sold some land, kept back some money, and then they got caught lying about it. Act 5:3 says, "But Peter said, 'Ananias, why has Satan filled your heart to lie to the Holy Spirit and keep back part of the price of the land for yourself?'" The key phrase is "for yourself," and God killed them.

Did God kill them just for lying? Don't we all lie at one time or another? Did He kill them to make an example of them? I think we would all be in trouble if that were the case. The answer is found with Simon the Sorcerer in Acts 8.

> And when Simon saw that through the laying on of the apostles' hands the Holy Spirit was given, he offered them money, saying, "Give me this power also, that anyone on whom I lay hands may receive the Holy Spirit." But Peter said to him, "Your money perish with you, because you thought that the gift of God could be purchased with money!" (Acts 8:18–20)

Purchasing the gift of God with money is the problem—greed and using God for worldly gain. Ananias and Sapphira perished with their money, and that would have been the same fate Simon was heading to before he was chastised and repented. Also notice that Achan perished with the money he hid in his tent. His money indeed did perish with him.

Matthew, Mark, and Luke repeat what Jesus said: "And again I say to you, it is easier for a camel to go through the eye of a needle than for a rich man to enter the kingdom of God." I have heard far too many times people explain this away by saying that He is talking about a camel walking through a city gate, or that it this doesn't say it is impossible for a rich man to get to heaven. People seem to try to find a lawyerly loophole in God's Word to explain their greed for money.

I can't help but think about the rich man who died and went to hell in Luke 16, and also the rich man in Mark 10 who asked Jesus about eternal life and went away sad because he had great possessions. Greedy people seem to forget that Jesus had nowhere to lay His head, and Peter had no silver or gold for the beggar in Acts. But here we are two thousand years later with men becoming rich off the Word of God. "Your money perish with you, because you thought that the gift of God could be purchased with money!"

I mentioned before that a certain church in the Houston, Texas, area makes seventy million dollars a year in donations. The leader of that church has many books written about living a great life now but fails to mention Christ and Him crucified in his motivational, charged messages. The biblical warnings are all there, and this would be the next stop on the apology tour. Jesus would have to say He is sorry to Achan, Ananias and his wife, and Simon the Sorcerer because He would not tolerate the zeal for money in Joshua and Acts, but now He is allowing it through these television charlatans.

Ravenous wolves? You betcha!

Is money bad? I am not advocating that it is. In Acts, the money was brought to the church for the needs of the church, and the best research I can do shows me that none of the seventy million dollars raked in by this Houston church goes to support a missionary or feed the hungry. I am more than willing to be shown where that money goes to help others in need if I am wrong. But to date, the best I can see is it seems the seventy million dollars go to Armani suits and polished, veneered teeth. "No one can serve two masters; for either he will hate the one and love the other, or else he will be loyal to the one and despise the other. You cannot serve God and mammon" (Matt. 6:24).

Next stop on the apology tour would be Aaron's sons, and the home of Eli and his sons, for worshiping incorrectly.

The sons of Aaron were church leaders, churchgoers, and priests. We are told in Leviticus 17:1–2, "Now the LORD spoke to Moses after the death of the two sons of Aaron, when they offered profane fire before the LORD, and died; and the LORD said to Moses: 'Tell Aaron your brother not to come at just any time into the Holy Place inside the veil, before the mercy seat which is on the ark, lest he die; for I will appear in the cloud above the mercy seat.'" God killed the sons of Aaron for worshiping incorrectly and even went so far as to tell the father of the priesthood, Aaron, that if he worshipped incorrectly, God would kill him too.

God must have held correct worship to a high standard then, as He does now. When we offer our worship to a holy God, it must be on His terms, not ours. If God says to lift holy hands, then we must lift holy hands. If God tells us to worship Him in spirit and truth, then our hearts and His truth have to be center stage.

Here is the story of Eli and his sons.

"Also the two sons of Eli, Hophni and Phinehas, the priests of the LORD, were there" (1 Sam. 1:3). Eli's sons were priests who took the offering from the people of Israel. Eli's sons were church leaders, churchgoers, and priests. "Now the sons of Eli were corrupt; they did not know the LORD." (1 Sam. 2:12). I know what you are thinking: "What? Priests who do not know the Lord?" Yep. They were out and about then, and they are out and about now. Maybe they are in your church. And God killed them. "Now this shall be a sign to you that will come upon your two sons, on Hophni and Phinehas: in one day they shall die, both of them" (1 Sam. 2:34). "Also the ark of God was captured; and the two sons of Eli, Hophni and Phinehas, died" (1 Sam. 4:11).

Why would God do such a thing? "Therefore the sin of the young men was very great before the LORD, for men abhorred the offering of the LORD" (1 Sam. 2:17). Abhorring the offering of the Lord is a big offense and should not be taken lightly or overlooked. If we have written direction from God as to how to worship and bring an offering, why should we change it? The killer of Abel, Cain, changed the offering, and God cast him out.

Worship to God correctly doesn't involve drinking poison, falling on the ground, or (as John Haggee puts it) screaming like a "Comanche Indian." Worshipping God is done on His terms, not the way I see it or how I feel. My feeling satisfied with my offering or elated in my emotions has to take a back seat to what God tells us to do. That brings me to one more stop on God's apology tour, and it starts with a pop quiz:

Pop Quiz: What if the supreme offering of the Lord?

The answer is Jesus. If you hate the sacrifice of the Lord, that being Jesus Christ, you would fall into the same predicament as the sons of Aaron and Eli. Yet to my wonderment, there are churches today who refuse to mention the cross or have it displayed in their church because people find it offensive. They fail to mention Jesus Christ because it drives people away, and they make no mention of the blood because of its upsetting tone. But they call themselves a Christian church.

I am not talking about some small, misguided church just outside of Podunk where they handle snakes and drink poison. I'm talking about huge churches with thousands attending. I am not going to mention names because I will be dismissed as a hater, but you may look for yourself with any search engine.

One church leader was asked how to build a megachurch in an interview. This man bragged that on an Easter Sunday, he spoke to sixty-seven thousand people, so I believe this man is qualified to speak on building a megachurch. He mentioned many things a church could do to increase attendance, but some of his advice particularly caught my attention.

He stated that he sent a group of people out into the neighborhood and asked the neighborhood what type of music they liked to listen to. It seemed that classic rock was a big response, so he brought that type of music into the church to draw in the people. I like classic rock (I grew up in the seventies), but I see a problem when we ask the world how to do church. It seemed the message given by standard songs like "Amazing Grace" and "The Old Rugged Cross" do not seem to get the toe tapping, so they are abandoned for U2 or The Beatles.

Another thing he mentioned was that people get confused and take offense to seeing a cross, so it is in the best interest of church growth to remove all crosses from view. Is the cross being available and visible in church a must? Maybe, maybe not. The issue is that when a church leader sees the cross as a negative thing, there is a problem. He forgets that convictions play a vital role in salvation, and the cross is convicting. That is why people find it offensive. Truth be told, I find it offensive. But truth be told again, I caused this offense!

I save the oddest megachurch building suggestion for last. This leader says that when you mention people are sinners, they don't hang around your church long, so it is best to not mention sin.

Maybe I am just an old antique who's hanging on to days gone by, but isn't the Bible about Jesus going to the cross because I am a sinner? Didn't Paul say in 2 Corinthians 2:12, "Furthermore, when I came to Troas to preach Christ's gospel, and a door was opened to me by the Lord," Christ's gospel? The last time I checked, the gospel of Christ is that He died for sinners … on the cross!

Paul also said in Galatians 1:8, "But even if we, or an angel from heaven, preach any other gospel to you than what we have preached to you, let him be accursed." Accursed? "No … How can this be? If I stood before sixty-seven thousand people on a Sunday, how could you dare put a curse on me?" Because you fail to preach the good news that Jesus went to the cross for sinners.

God would have to apologize to the sons of Aaron, the sons of Eli, and those whom He killed for worshiping incorrectly (see Korah, his family, and two thousand people in Exodus). God would also have to apologize to those old archaic Bible writers like Paul, Peter, and John, who put so much faith in the cross, blood, and the forgiveness of sin. When they wrote, the apostles thought it was everything! But today, it drives good tithing people out of the church, so we had better keep the cross, sin, and the blood to ourselves, and maybe we can whisper about it later in back rooms.

Is Jesus coming on the clouds in a glorious, victorious manner to take His children home? Or is He coming hat in hand with His eyes to the ground, humbled by television hucksters and a politically correct church? Will Jesus come to humans apologizing and saying that He has learned the errors of His ways, with a promise to go back and rewrite the Bible to be more pleasing to the needs of modern people?

How could the God of creation, who can see the end and the beginning at the same time, suddenly say, "Now is the time for me to change my mind. Thus sayeth the Lord!" God Himself would be in violation of Deuteronomy 4 and Revelation 22, and He would have to rewrite Psalm 138:2 because He doesn't lift His Word above His name after all.

Jesus is the same yesterday, today, and forever, and the Word does not change. The Word of God is the best recipe to bake a cake in the history of humankind, and there is no reason to try to bake it your way by adding extra sugar to sweeten it and removing the eggs because PETA is picketing your church.

Stick to the recipe!

Chapter 7

Men Are from Earth; Paul Is from Mars Hill

B efore I entered the ministry, I wore many hats, and one particular cap was that of a corrections officer in the state of Nevada. I had worked there for a few years, and from that position, I left and turned fully to seeking a pastorate.

I worked in the northern part of the state, and our particular prison was in charge of accepting all new convicted inmates into the Nevada prison system. It didn't matter whether a person had committed a murder or was a tax cheat. If you had been convicted of a crime and went to prison, it was a good chance my face was one of the first one you saw.

Each person entering Nevada's prison system has to go through a few assessments before they begin to do their time. They are checked for health issues, gang affiliation, escape risk, and violent tendencies, and from these assessments, it is determined which of the five prisons in Nevada they will do their time. To these means, it was my job to hold the shotgun just in case.

Officers keep their distance from inmates, both physically and personally. We cannot take the time to befriend any of the thousands of inmates entering into our prison, and a motto of "Firm, Fair, and Consistent" is one of our battle cries as we endeavor to treat each prisoner with dignity and consistency. Being a friend to any of the inmates can be disastrous and dangerous, so there has to be a distance between the officers and inmates.

As each inmate is brought into the process of assessment, this can takes up to two weeks. And as each inmate is evaluated, the individual prisoners are held in small cells, about ten feet by fifteen feet with a steel frame, that have a shelf with padding as a bed, a wool blanket, a sink, and a commode. No windows, save the small slit of wired glass on the door so each officer can check on the safety of the newly arrived inmates. No personal items are brought in—no snack food, no love letters, nothing from home. Nothing from the outside world is allowed while each man awaits his next point of incarceration.

Each cell is equipped with an intercom system that the inmate can use if he needs something, such as medical assistance or a personal mental health evaluation. The intercom is not used like the front desk of a hotel, but we understand that the first few hours and days of incarceration are the hardest on a man, and we are trained to understand that the first twenty-four hours of prison are the highest for suicide and breakdowns.

After we safely secured all new inmates to their cells, I received a light on my intercom panel from one of the younger inmates. I asked him in that firm, fair, and consistent voice, "What do you need?"

This small voice reached up and said, *"Officer Hall, can I have something to read?"*

My usual response was that they would only be in intake for a short period of time, and he would find many things to read when he got to the prison he was assigned.

I didn't say that this day. This day, I told the inmate with the mousy voice, *"I will see what I can do."*

Officers cannot bring reading material into the prison because we are paid to watch and protect, not read and sleep. I could not go to another inmate somewhere else, ask him for some reading material, and then give it to the young inmate because I would then be indebted to an inmate for a magazine. I would then be in a compromising position with both inmates. I would owe one inmate a debt of gratitude, and the other inmate would think that corrections officers are personal porters ready to do all that is asked. As you can see, even as a Christian, we are sometimes held to the standards of the employer even when we want to do a good thing for a person.

Before these new inmates arrived, I had helped a detail with cleaning out the cells of accumulated trash and other inmate belongings. As we wait for new inmates, the cells are often used to hold unruly inmates or inmates being release or transferring off the yard. Inmates who have already been through the process of intake into the prison can have personal belongings. While helping in the cleanup process, I found a state-issued King James Bible and had taken it to my loft. I was reading it after the inmates were secured.

Inmates can have religious material at any time, and prison rules are discussed with inmates at the end of their two weeks in intake. This young inmate wasn't aware that he could have a Bible. The process is that when you arrive at your assigned prison, you may write a request for a Bible. This is about a four-week process.

On my break, I walked to the cell where the young man was and slid the Bible under the door. Through the small slit window, I could see enough in the dark cell that he picked it up. I told him that he should start with the Gospel of John.

There are very few things a Christian corrections officer can do for an inmate. We have to refrain from deep conversation about Christ and salvation for the main fact that we cannot watch fifty inmates while we are trying to lead one to salvation. If I am spending quality time with one young convert, two other inmates may be fighting or harming others. As much as we may love people, we corrections officers have to maintain a distance not only for our own safety but for the safety of others.

A corrections officer would lose his job if he were to take the time to take an inmate by the hands and pray with him. Not only is the loss of his job, but there also the safety concerns. An officer cannot take the time to organize a Bible study, open an inmate meal with prayer, or show any favoritism; otherwise, he would break his vow of being firm, fair, and consistent. By giving this new inmate a Bible, I could have opened up a can of worms. I had fifty inmates at the time and only one Bible. What if all the men yelled, "Where is mine?" You see the potential problems. However, this young, squeaky inmate was in his rights to have a Bible, and I stayed with in my job description by giving him a prison-issue Bible. It was what I could do at the moment.

Two years later, I was working a little overtime in the front of the prison. I don't care too much for overtime—not because of the work, but because I have always been busier away from where I work and need that time away. However, I was asked if I could come in and help, so I agreed. When any inmate finishes his sentence, we don't simply open the door. He is processed out like a soldier being given his release, and I was helping with the release of eight inmates.

A young man came up to me and said, "Officer Hall, do you remember me?"

I have to confess I did not remember him. I saw thousands of inmates and could not remember this one, so I had to tell him, "No, son, I don't remember you."

He said, "You saved my life." I had to ask if I had broken up a fight he was in, or if I may have fired a shot at someone going to harm him.

He said that two years ago, he had determined that when the judge had sentenced him to prison, when he arrived here, he was going to kill himself the first night he got a cell. It was this young, squeaky-voiced kid I had given that Bible to, and now he was a little older and wiser. He said that he read the Gospel of John, and when he started, he couldn't put it down and changed his mind about suicide. That small act of giving a Bible and giving direction saved his life.

I never really saw his young face through the small slit dark window, and I never kept up with his progress in prison. I did what I could with what I had, and it changed this young man's life. I didn't read John 3:16 to him or take him down the Romans road. One small act in one small minute, in one small arena, was all it took. He told me that he had been in touch with a church on the outside, and he was being picked up by one of the church members. He was ready to begin a new life—one with Jesus Christ.

I felt that true story, and this middle chapter needed to be written now because so far, most of what we have seen is bad news with ravenous wolf false teachers, Balaamites, apostates, and those in the church who feel that God has changed His mind about sin and now seem to think we can build churches around what had gotten others killed.

How about some good news? How about those who look beyond denominations and do the work of the Jesus Christ without asking the question, "So, where do you go to church?"

The story I opened the chapter with is very much true; this actually happened to me and this young man. The truth also is that to this day, I cannot remember his name. He didn't give it to me at our brief encounter as he was leaving prison, hopefully for good. As a matter of fact, if I added up all the time I had spent with his young man who may have made just one bad choice in his life, we spent about two minutes together: one minute for me to give him a Bible and a little direction, and one minute two years later for him to say thanks and give his testimony.

There was no beautiful building for us to enter, no altars for us to pray at, no Sunday school class at ten in the morning, and no baptismal to use. Just one squeaky-voiced young man accepting the heartfelt gift given by another man who loves Jesus Christ. I didn't ask him if he were Baptist, Pentecostal, or Methodist because it didn't matter to us. What we had shared—one old, preowned Bible and the Gospel of John—will forever link us. I imagine that I will get his name as we approach the throne that day, and maybe we can cast our crowns at the feet of Jesus together.

Pop Quiz: Who is qualified to preach the gospel?

You are qualified to preach the gospel. There are many, many ways we can reach out and impact people for the Lord, and the two-minute fellowship between me and this young man is a good example. If I were to mention some names to you of warriors for the Lord, I believe all would recognize them. The names of Billy Graham and Mother Theresa are our present-day heroes of faith.

Billy Graham went from town to town preaching the good news of Jesus Christ. I am sure he attended a home church for rest and fellowship, as we all should, but he took the Word to the streets. I see Greg Laurie doing this today, carrying the torch. I don't believe either man has opened up the arenas of the world to a great Catholic evangelical movement or a call for Baptists only.

There are no signs at the door that say, "Welcome, all members of the Assembly of God" or "Good evening, fellow Lutherans." These men, and others like them, come to different towns bringing the fresh waters of the Gospel to a dry and thirsty land.

I never read an account of Mother Theresa where it said that she only served Catholics or demanded conversion before she helped them. I am friends with a group in Charlotte, North Carolina, called Serving in Missions (SIM), and they plant missionaries all over the world. When you fill out a request to serve, they asked about your relationship with Jesus Christ, not whether you go to a confessional or speak in languages. This group and other missions like them are concerned with spreading to truth of Jesus. Adding to local church attendance is not their goal, and it shouldn't be ours.

These people go out into the world from Charlotte to Calcutta to reach the lost. Apostle Paul was like that. In his dusty, tattered, and worn leather sandals, I am confident that if Paul said that his thorn in the flesh was fallen arches in his feet, we would fully understand why he asked God to remove the thorn. Paul went everywhere all the time. To stop Paul, they had to arrest him, and he stilled reached the lost from prison with letters.

Paul did what he could with what he had and used his surroundings to witness to people. I said in the title of the chapter that Paul was from Mars Hill, and it is this clever little point of understanding that Paul gives us that I want us to ponder.

In Acts 17, we have a story of Paul in Greece, and he has gotten the attention of those smart, aristocratic brainiacs and religious people in the Athens area. They wanted to at least hear what Paul had to say. Most people, even today, worship their own minds and intellect and feel that the truth of God is open to how they construe it, not realizing that God's truth is not open to how any person personally interprets it. But these men in Greece then were no different than most people today.

As Paul entered into the area, he had observed many altars in the area with inscriptions to the gods of these intelligent people. Maybe an altar to Vol, the god of the sun, or an altar to Asheroth or Baal, and those other Old Testament gods we read about. Altars to a god of the sea, a god of the air, and a god of the dirt were seen everywhere. Looking at my personality, I would have been upset and gone in yelling and screaming while I kicked all the altars over and demanded that they beg forgiveness and seek Christ. Paul didn't do that.

After seeing all these altars, this happened: "Then Paul stood in the midst of the Areopagus and said, 'Men of Athens, I perceive that in all things you are very religious'" (Acts 17:22). He saw these people for who they were, not who he wanted them to be. If we cannot look at people and see them for who they are, we will lose them. We need to see each man as a person created by God who is lost until Jesus enters his or her life. If I had kicked over every altar in Greece and screamed the name of Jesus, I doubt any would have been saved. Paul saw them for who they were and tried to reach them on their terms, not his.

Paul did what he could with what he had, and after telling these men he understood them, he said this:

> For as I was passing through and considering the objects of your worship, I even found an altar with this inscription:
>
> TO THE UNKNOWN GOD.
>
> Therefore, the One whom you worship without knowing, Him I proclaim to you. (Acts 17:23)

Paul saw those in Athens as men who recognized deity and were seeking divine guidance. Paul said, "I am just like you." He used what was at his disposal to reach these people right where they were.

The common thread between all men is sin, and if we can look at the lost and show them that the sickness that infects all humankind has a cure, then we can reach those who are just like us. We are all sinners saved by grace; we have all fallen short of God and His glory. This puts us all on a level surface, and this is where we start. Denominations, church buildings, and services at 11:00 a.m. are not what saves people. Common people spreading the Good News is what does it.

Paul continued to speak to them, and after these people saw a common thread, they were open to what Paul had to say. "God, who made the world and everything in it, since He is Lord of heaven and earth, does not dwell in temples made with hands. Nor is He worshiped with men's hands, as though He needed anything, since He gives to all life, breath, and all things" (Acts 17:24–25). Paul tells him that God does not live in statues, altars, or (in our present times) church buildings. We sing a song, "Surely the Presence of the Lord Is in This Place," and that song should be sung from Charlotte to Calcutta, in your home, at Walmart, and everywhere the name of the Lord is spoken.

I can hear the critics now. "Sure, that was the apostle Paul. And I ain't Billy Graham." But please realize that neither am I when I took the time to do what I could by giving a young man a Bible. Paul had a first message at one time. So did Billy Graham and Mother Theresa. When will your first message be?

Chapter 8

The Good

I am a bivocational pastor and work part-time for the USPS. I use my own vehicles when delivering the mail. It pays in the long run to maintain the vehicles you drive, and going a little further in vehicle upkeep can save you time, energy, and frustration.

I buy six- and eight-ply tires that cost more, but when you are out on a long, dirty, unpaved road and have a flat tire, it is then that you wish you had spent the extra money on good tires. Oil changes and new brakes are given in some cases on a monthly basis because your vehicle is your moneymaker. And keep your receipts, just in case something goes wrong.

I needed new windshield wipers, and because I need the clearest view possible at all times and this vehicle needs to run at peak service at all times, I went all out and bought the expensive wipers that had all the bells and whistles. These wipers were three blades in one that could push wet cement off the windshield if you needed them to. Nothing could stand in their way, and in order to meet the demands of snow, rain, heat, or gloom of night, you need good wipers.

After paying the nearly twenty dollars, the attendant in the auto store asked if I wanted him to take the old wipers off and put the new one on the car. "No," I said, "I think I am capable of installing these" I walked out and drove home. When I arrived in the safe confines of my own driveway, I took off the old, one-blade, wipers and installed my new, state-of-the-art, top-of-the-line, glow-in-the-dark (maybe I'm stretching it) wipers on my car. The old one popped off easily, and the new one went on just as easy. It wasn't raining that day, and I didn't test out the new wipers. Besides, do you test out new tires, or do you simply trust them when you drive away from the tire shop? I trusted the wipers.

A few days later, I found that there was a slight mist in the morning as I went off to deliver the mail, so I turned on my new "conquer the world" wipers. All they could do was smear the water on my windshield. The mist became a drizzle, and as the water fell, my new wipers moved the water from one side of the windshield to the other like an oily mess of goop. I couldn't see out of the windshield and was forced to drive in the rain with my head out of the window because my windshield view was useless.

When I finally got the chance to address the problem of the new wipers, I saw that there was a thin, clear protective sheath put across the three blades to protect the three rubber blades while being stored in its box. When I removed the sheath, the wipers worked better than any wiper I had ever purchased.

To tell you the truth, I didn't read the directions, which I am sure would have said, "Remove protective sheath before operating world-conquering wipers." That brings me to this biblical analogy: When you read the directions from the beginning, you will have every opportunity for the clearest possible view in the future.

I am entitling the next three small chapters as "The Good," "The Bad," and "The Ugly" because when people get involved in God's church, we can do good things, bad things, and downright ugly things, all in the name of church.

Again, this book is a call for Christians to unite together in harmony for Jesus. I am not advocating leaving your buildings or forming another group. I am saying that we must drop all the things that separate us and cling to Jesus, because He is the church. We need to, as His church, bond together and obey what He tells us. I believe Satan wins a great victory if he can keep us separated and distant from all other believers.

> Though you have not seen Him, you love Him,
> and though you do not see Him now, but believe
> in Him, you greatly rejoice with joy inexpressible
> and full of glory. (1 Pet. 1:8)

We have not seen Christ face-to-face as Peter did, but our fellowship can be genuine because it is marked by love, trust, and obedience. The love Peter speaks of in 1 Peter 1:8 isn't shallow emotionalism or sentimentality. It's the love of the will—the love of choice. His readers had chosen to love Christ despite never having seen Him physically. Such love is marked by obedience, as Jesus affirms: "If you love Me, you will keep My commandments … He who does not love Me does not keep My words" (John 14:15, 24). To have fellowship with Christ is to love and obey Him.

We choose to do all things because God gave each of us a will, and a free will at that. We have the freedom of will to choose to do well or to do badly. When we sin, we choose to sin; no other person makes us sin. When we do what is right, we make that choice. "I call heaven and earth as witnesses today against you, that I have set before you life and death, blessing and cursing; therefore choose life, that both you and your descendants may live" (Deut. 30:19). Life itself is a series of choices, and our choices extend to life and death. We should choose life.

People choose life when they accept the atoning work of Jesus Christ on the cross. As we look at what Jesus says about His church in Revelation 2 and 3, please understand that there is no advocacy for salvation by works, or what a person does. God's Word is clear that we are saved by His grace and that alone (Acts 15:11, Eph. 2:5, 8; 2 Tim. 1:19).

There is, however, a way we should live that shows our faith, and that is what Jesus will judge us by in Revelation. James 2:26 says, "For as the body without the spirit is dead, so faith without works is dead also." We should see that our faith is alive when we act out what we believe. We are not called to sit back and do nothing after we are saved. We are not called by God to warm a seat a couple hours a week "in His name." I believe the Newsboys put it best in their song "Beautiful Sound" when Peter Furler sings,

> To have found You, and still be looking for You,
> It's "the soul's paradox of love."
> You fill my cup, I lift it up for more.
> I won't stop now that I'm free.
> I'll be chasing You
> like You chase me.

We do not stop our movement with God because we get saved. It is not a finishing point to life–it is a starting point. After all. isn't called a walk?

I want us to take a look at Revelation 2 and 3 with human choice in mind. In Revelation, we see that Jesus will judge the Church someday. He will not judge buildings or denominations as a whole; He will judge those individual believers who have made the choice to follow Him. He gives us praise for the good choices His Church has made, and He gives warnings for the bad choices His Church has made.

As we look at these choices, my sarcasm got the best of me, and I entitled these next three chapters "The Good," "The Bad," and "The Ugly" after the old Clint Eastwood movie because we can make good choices, bad choices, and downright ugly choices. Because Jesus addressed His churches in Revelation 2–3 with the good things they did first, I will too. I have condensed the good choices into one chapter and the bad into another chapter. Then we will address the ugly in a separate chapter.

Here are the good things Jesus addresses in Revelation 2–3, condensed.

> I know your works, your labor, your patience, and that you cannot bear those who are evil. And you have tested those who say they and have found them liars; and you have persevered and have patience, and have labored for My name's sake and have not become weary. (Rev. 2:2–3)

> I know your works, tribulation, and poverty (but you are rich); Do not fear any of those things which you are about to suffer. Indeed, the devil is about to throw some of you into prison, that you may be tested, and you will have tribulation ten days. Be faithful until death, and I will give you the crown of life. (Rev 2:9–10)

> I know your works, and where you dwell, where Satan's throne is. And you hold fast to My name, and did not deny My faith even in the days in which Antipas was My faithful martyr, who was killed among you, where Satan dwells. (Rev. 2:13)

> I know your works, love, service, faith, and your patience; and as for your works, the last are more than the first. (Rev. 2:19)

> But hold fast what you have till I come. And he who overcomes, and keeps My works until the end, to him I will give power over the nations. (Rev. 2:25–26)

Be watchful, and strengthen the things which remain, that are ready to die, for I have not found your works perfect before God. Remember therefore how you have received and heard; hold fast and repent. Therefore if you will not watch, I will come upon you as a thief, and you will not know what hour I will come upon you. You have a few names even in Sardis who have not defiled their garments; and they shall walk with Me in white, for they are worthy. He who overcomes shall be clothed in white garments, and I will not blot out his name from the Book of Life; but I will confess his name before My Father and before His angels. (Rev. 3:2–5)

I know your works. See, I have set before you an open door, and no one can shut it; for you have a little strength, have kept My word, and have not denied My name … Because you have kept My command to persevere, I also will keep you from the hour of trial which shall come upon the whole world, to test those who dwell on the earth. Behold, I am coming quickly! Hold fast what you have, that no one may take your crown. (Rev. 3:8, 10–11)

The good we can do for God and the causes of Jesus Christ are some really, really good things. The problem I see with church today is that we wait until hurting people come into our buildings before we feel we can help. We treat church sometimes like a car commercial, and we try to sell our buildings and services instead of reaching out to the hurting. Today's church commercial would seem to be, "Come on down to Southern Pentecostal Assembly of the Saint of the Great Membership this Sunday for fun, fellowship, and that feel-good experience, as only we at SPASM can do. Where we move for Him … voluntary and involuntary."

Our focus seems to be on the church structure, what people will feel, the building and its services, and the time we can help. We are not going out to reach the lost. The point is that we are to go into the world and reach the lost, not to expect that a building will do that. Church is an outreach into the world, not a call to a corner. When we claim a corner and do that, the church becomes a scene from *The Warriors*, where each gangs claims turf and you are encouraged to join them at their given time.

Let us look at the good Jesus mentions and understand that there is no street corner that has restricted our choice to do well.

The first good things Jesus mentions in Revelation is this: "know your works, your labor, your patience, and that you cannot bear those who are evil. And you have tested those who say they are apostles and are not and have found them liars." Jesus commends this group of believers who have pointed out evildoers and false teachers in the church. If there are evildoers in the church, we are not supposed to try to understand their evil. We are not supposed to try to get inside their minds and assess their childhood issues or problem marriages as to why they do evil. We are supposed to have nothing to do with them (Rom. 16:17). Jesus also commends those who recognize false teachers.

Pop Quiz: How can you test a false teacher or leader?

You can test a false teacher by the Word. Jesus, in the judgment, will commend us for not putting up with false teachers and evildoers in the church. We will see in the next chapter that those who allow false prophets in the Church will be chastised.

Then there is tribulation ("I know your works, tribulation, and poverty") and those who are faithful to the end, which is a call for all of us to hold fast to the truths of Jesus Christ and to not waver when faced with peer pressure, honest persecution, and poverty even to the point of death. Stand fast!

"Love, service, faith, and your patience and he who overcomes, and keeps My works until the end, to him I will give power over the nations" (Rev. 2:19, 25–26). Please see the attitude of these believers: love, faith, patience, overcome. These are people who do more than talk the talk—they walk the walk!

Jesus commends these believers more for who they are in their hearts than what they have done. They have kept His works, and that can be boiled down to us as "love the Lord and love thy neighbor." This is why Jesus says that they have done good. With their attitude alone, the attitude isn't a reflection of any denomination.

Next up is this passage: "Remember therefore how you have received and heard; hold fast and repent. Therefore if you will not watch, I will come upon you as a thief."

Pop Quiz: Remember what?

The answer is what you have received and heard. The Word!

Finally, we come to this verse: "See, I have set before you an open door." Most would see this as a missions-minded group, and I will agree. However, our mission field is located just outside the door of your own home. It is not the responsibility of a building to lead people to Jesus Christ. That responsibility is yours and mine. Every believer has the responsibility to tell people about Jesus (Mark 16:15). Jesus is the door (John 10), and He commends those who have told the lost about Him.

I remember talking to a loved one who had told me that she met a man in a Walmart whom she used to work with, and this man had fallen on hard times. He was drinking heavily and doing drugs. My friend said she told him he needed to get in church. That is the wrong answer. What she should have done was introduce him to Jesus Christ, right there in Walmart. Why should we depend on the local church building to do what you and I have been called to do?

We should all be bold enough to tell people how wonderful Jesus has been to us. We should choose to speak up for Him, and we should choose to do all the good things Jesus commends His church for in Revelation.

I encourage you to reread the quotations assembled concerning the good things for which Jesus will judge His church. Read it again and see how you, as an individual, measure up. The good that we are judged for is not because we go to a church building or follow church tradition. It is a measure of the heart toward Jesus and His Church.

James tells us several things in his book.

> Do not be deceived, my beloved brethren. (James 1:16)
> But do you want to know, O foolish man, that faith without works is dead? (James 2:20)
> But be doers of the word, and not hearers only, deceiving yourselves. (James 1:22)

That is great advice from the brother of our Lord and Savior.

We will all stand before the Lord someday in judgment, and our choices will allow Jesus to say, "Well done, good and faithful servant; you were faithful over a few things, I will make you ruler over many things. Enter into the joy of your lord" (Matt. 25:21).

Chapter 9

The Bad

I was told the story of an Italian millionaire who was a collector of fine art and other expensive things, and he passed away after a long illness. When his next of kin came to collect the belongings in his home, it was discovered that along with the countless expensive knickknacks in his attic, he had also collected over 250 violins from all over the world.

The man was an aficionado on violins and collected every one that he could buy. Most were what we would call run-of-the-mill types, although he did have some that were very expensive.

It was said by the commentator that when the violins were discovered, it seemed the millionaire's final legacy would be that in his greed by hiding away these treasures, he denied the world the opportunity to enjoy the sweet music that only these violins could play.

I see that attitude in most believers. It is as if when they have excepted Christ and hear the beautiful music that only He can play in their lives, most bundle this priceless treasure away in their hearts the way that the millionaire stowed away the violins, telling no one and denying the world the sweet music that was meant for everybody. They keep it only for themselves.

We choose to either yell out about Jesus or keep silent. We give the world our embrace, or we show them our embarrassment. "For I am not ashamed of the gospel of Christ" (Rom. 1:16).

Chapter 8 was what Jesus has commended the Church on and what we will receive a crown for. This brief chapter will show us what Jesus said specifically to the Church about bad behavior and choices that we (the Church) have made. Again, I have condensed this into one collection with hopes that it can be read as a warning in and by itself.

"Nevertheless I have this against you, that you have left your first love. Remember therefore from where you have fallen; repent and do the first works, or else I will come to you quickly and remove your lampstand from its place—unless you repent. (Rev. 2:4–5)

I have a few things against you, because you have their who hold the doctrine of Balaam, who taught Balak to put a stumbling block before the children of Israel, to eat things sacrificed to idols, and to commit sexual immorality. (Rev. 2:14)

I have a few things against you, because you allow that woman Jezebel, who calls herself a prophetess, to teach and seduce My servants to commit sexual immorality and eat things sacrificed to idols. And

> I gave her time to repent of her sexual immorality, and she did not repent. Indeed I will cast her into a sickbed, and those who commit adultery with her into great tribulation, unless they repent of their deeds. (Rev. 2:20–24)

> I know your works, that you have a name that you are alive, but you are dead. (Rev. 3:1)

> I know your works, that you are neither cold nor hot. I could wish you were cold or hot. So then, because you are lukewarm, and neither cold nor hot, will I vomit you out of My mouth. Because you say, "I am rich, have become wealthy, and have need of nothing"—and do not know that you are wretched, miserable, poor, blind, and naked—I counsel you to buy from Me gold refined in the fire, that you may be rich; and white garments, that you may be clothed, that the shame of your nakedness may not be revealed; and anoint your eyes with eye salve, that you may see. As many as I love, I rebuke and chasten. Therefore be zealous and repent. (Rev. 3:15–19)

As you can see, there is plenty going on to have our Lord and Savior upset at us, the Church. I need to point out that these good and bad deeds are ongoing issues all the way until the end, when Jesus returns for us. We find the word *repent* thirty-three times in the Bible, and ten of those are in the book of Revelation. Jesus will point out what we are doing wrong and asks us to turn from those bad things by repenting.

Pop Quiz: How do I repent?

Repent means "to change one's mind," or to turn and go in another direction. This is a choice made by those who have fallen into the sins that Jesus rebukes in Revelation. To repent is as easy as seeing that I am doing something wrong and going in a wrong direction, and then making a mindful decision to stop the wrong and head in the right direction. It is as easy as making the right choice.

The first thing Jesus addresses is those who "have left your first love," and I think we can agree that we see this all the time in the Church. It is as if when we come to the Lord and give Him our lives, we have this fire in our hearts for Him, and we can't seem to get enough of Him. After time, like a nova that is burning bright through the sky, the fire dims, fades, and then seems to go out. Maybe our expectations were not met, and maybe our flame burns out. For whatever reason, Jesus reminds us to make the choice to reignite that fire and turn back to our first love.

"Those who hold the doctrine of Balaam." Balaam was addresses in the fourth chapter of this book when we met apostates, and Balaam sold out Israel for money. Balaam gave advice to Balak to have the Moabite women seduce the Israelite men to marry out their race and have sex with these non-Jewish women. We are told, "Do not be unequally yoked together with unbelievers. For what fellowship has righteousness with lawlessness? And what communion has light with darkness?" and Balaam sold out Israel to be unequally yoked with heathens. This is great advice to all believers: Do not marry an unbeliever or commit sexually unclean acts. If you are not committed to a one-person sexual relationship with your believing spouse, start now.

After addressing this behavior with the church of Pergamos, Jesus continues on the theme of sexual purity by addressing this issue alone to the church of Thyatira accusing them of allowing that woman Jezebel to seduce them into sexual impurity. Do you think that if Jesus chastises two groups for the same issue He wants us to pay good attention to the problem? Stay sexually pure.

"I know your works, that you have a name that you are alive, but you are dead" (Rev. 3:1). Some see this as a group that has no emotional fervor for the things of God, and I think this can be true, however I would like to ask a question.

Pop Quiz: If these people are dead, what is life?

Speaking of Jesus, John said in John 1:4, "In Him was life, and the life was the light of men." Jesus also said, "I am the way, the truth, and the life" (John 14:6). Could it be that there are churchgoers who do not have this life?

Let me take a moment to mention to you that these seven churches that Jesus is asking to repent are all churchgoing people. Let that sink in for a moment. Churchgoing people who, on Sunday morning, sing the songs, open in prayer, write a tithe check, listen to the message, and even sometimes laugh at the preacher's jokes. These are the ones Jesus is chastising in Revelation 2–3. And this is not the first time.

In Matthew 7:22–23, Jesus said that not everyone who says "Lord, Lord" to Him will end up in heaven. "Many will say to Me in that day, 'Lord, Lord, have we not prophesied in Your name, cast out demons in Your name, and done many wonders in Your name?' And then I will declare to them, 'I never knew you; depart from Me, you who practice lawlessness!'" And these people do these things where? In church!

Where else do you prophesy (preach) in the name of Jesus? Where else do you cast out demons (pray for people) in the name of Jesus? Where else do you do wonders (speaking in tongues, etc.) in the name of Jesus? These are churchgoing people who do not know Jesus Christ in a personal, intimate relationship, and when they stand before Him on judgment day, the only thing they will hear is, "I never knew you; depart from Me," unless they take His advice now and repent.

Jesus tells us that there are dead people in His Church—pretenders who are playing with their very future in heaven who need to stop talking the talk and start walking the walk. We are asked by Paul in 2 Corinthians 13:5 to "Examine yourselves as to whether you are in the faith. Test yourselves. Do you not know yourselves, that Jesus Christ is in you?—unless indeed you are disqualified." I have to ask: who in the church does that?

Sometimes I feel we are afraid to look in the mirror and see who we really are. We avoid self-examination because we know what we will find. We don't examine ourselves because ignorance is bliss, and if we are happy with our meager walk and are happy just getting by with milk, why should we look any deeper into our relationship with God?

Philippians 2:12 tells us to "work out your own salvation with fear and trembling," and this is an ongoing process. I guess the real question is this: Do you want to be sure of your salvation? And do you want to be a more perfect person now than you were yesterday? This comes from self-examination. Our salvation is fluid, not a finished point.

I think we should all be afraid of what Jesus told the five foolish virgins who were waiting their entire lives for Jesus with Bible in hand, and when He came, they were shut out and told, "Assuredly, I say to you, I do not know you" (Matt. 25). This is the most frightening passage in the Bible. To be waiting for Jesus and looking for Him, and when He comes, it is then you find out you are dead, and He never knew you. Examine yourself before it is too late.

Then there are those pretenders who "are neither cold nor hot." I have a question for all who read this book and have made it this far: Why can't you live for Jesus twenty-four seven?

This book is not about doing away with buildings or traditions. It is about His believers coming together every moment we can for God. Whether we are Baptists, Pentecostals, Catholics, or Lutherans, we can live our lives for God by being hot for Him every moment of every day, but we cannot do this alone. We were never made to be alone, and now we are part of His Church. We are many members in one body, and we need to embrace that—and not embrace it solely on Sunday mornings or Wednesday evenings on a particular street corner, but every moment. We can do this, if we choose to.

Before we get to the ugly in the next chapter, I want us to see some other passages in Revelation 2–3. Twice we are told about the Nicolaitans, once in Revelation 2:6 and again in 2:15.

> But this you have, that you hate the deeds of the Nicolaitans, which I also hate. (Rev. 2:6)
> Thus you also have those who hold the doctrine of the Nicolaitans, which thing I hate. (Rev. 2:15)

Without me going into a college course on the Nicolaitans, they are simply this: those who have brought the things of this world into the Church. The Nicolaitans are those who have taken what they have learned and heard and added the things of the world to that. Jesus mentions them twice, so I feel I had to address it. God says twice that this is something He hates. Keep the world out of the Church.

"To him who overcomes I will give some of the hidden manna to eat. And I will give him a white stone, and on the stone a new name written which no one knows except him who receives it" (Rev. 2:17)." We make the choice to overcome sin or unrighteous living and walking the wrong walk. We choose to overcome, and we will be rewarded. As the old sage used to say, "Stick to the plan, Stan." Overcome.

Another choice we make is right here in Revelation 3:20–21, "Behold, I stand at the door and knock. If anyone hears My voice and opens the door, I will come in to him and dine with him, and he with Me. To him who overcomes I will grant to sit with Me on My throne, as I also overcame and sat down with My Father on His throne."

After all the bad that the Lord addresses to the Church in Revelation 2–3, He still offers us a choice to repent and turn to Him. We choose to hear His voice, open the door, and invite Jesus in. We overcome. He knocks, and we open. He knocks for everyone, but it is a shame that most don't want to open the door. I pray that you choose to open the door.

Chapter 10

The Ugly

I spent the yearly years of my life just outside Detroit, Michigan, before moving to the South, and I have to say that how a conversation is started differs from the North and the South. I have found that in the North, it is common to open a first-time conversation with somebody with "So what do you do for a living?" or "Where do you work?" That is the question that seems to break the ice. People in the North are direct and to the point who don't spend a great deal of time beating around bushes.

People in the South are very likely to ask a stranger, "So where do you go to church?" This comes out in such a natural way that you don't feel pressured or offended. It's a Bible Belt kind of thing, I guess. People in the North are firmly direct, whereas people from the South are more warmly pointed with both trying to find out where you are in life, with employment and church both playing major parts.

We sum each other up by what we do for a living and the type of church we attend. It is not rocket science, just a meager measuring stick. However, gossip isn't a Northern or Southern thing—it is a people thing.

Because I was raised in the North and replanted myself in the South, I see things a little differently. In the North, churchgoers are not afraid to tell you what is on their minds, even if it is the business of another church attendee. If a person is having an affair on his wife, a person in the North will say, "See him? He is stepping out on his wife," and they will let it fly regardless of being a gossip.

I have found that gossip in the South has become a subtle art. Gossip in the South is called sharing and caring, and you can always tell when people are going to gossip because they begin the conversation with, "Bless her heart," and then we learn about so-and-so. "Gertrude, bless her heart … That man is running around on her again." "Did you hear about Tom, bless his heart? They came and repossessed his car."

Being concerned about people is not a Northern or Southern thing. It is a God thing, and we should be concerned about Gertrude and Tom. That is normal and natural. However, we need to set aside the need to talk about other people's problems without them being there. We need to stop gossiping and talking about people, even if we think we are doing it in the name of love, good intentions, or justice.

I want to begin this by saying that God still loves the ugly. I have been ugly at times, and He still loves me. My sins and the sins of all believers are ugly to Him, and He still went so far as to come and rescue us on the cross. God does ugly.

But God somehow looks beyond the act and embraces the actor. In this chapter, we will see things that God hates and things that He find abominable, and through it all, God still loves the ugly.

Now, on to the ugly things that happen in church. Jesus directly addresses His Church in Revelation 2–3 about the good the Church does and the bad, but there is another passage of scripture I want us to see regarding what God sees as ugly among His people.

Pop Quiz: Can God see the good, the bad, and also the ugly?

The writer of Proverbs 6 speaks in a kind of riddle by starting his proverb by saying God hates six things, but then the writer lists seven issues. The writer says that number seven is an "abomination to Him," so let us take a look at the difference between things God hate and a thing He find as an abomination to Him.

> These six things the Lord hates,
> Yes, seven are an abomination to Him:
> A proud look,
> A lying tongue,
> Hands that shed innocent blood,
> A heart that devises wicked plans,
> Feet that are swift in running to evil,
> A false witness who speaks lies,
> And one who sows discord among brethren. (Prov. 6:16–19)

The six things God hates falls under the category of the no-brainer to common people and also those in His kingdom. We shouldn't be arrogant, lie, shed innocent blood, devise wicked plans, run to evil, or speak falsehood. We can read this and say, "Of course we shouldn't do those things." God gave the Ten Commandments to everybody, not just the Church.

First is a proud look. If I were to stand in the middle of a shopping mall with a clipboard and asked people to take the time to answer the question "Do you like arrogant people who look down on others?" I don't believe I would get many people to say, "Yes, arrogant people really are the kind of people I admire." We don't seem to get a warm and fuzzy feeling about those proud people who show their snobbery. We don't care for those types of people, whether in the mall, at work, or in church. God hates this also, so we are in excellent company.

Number two on the list is a lying tongue, and we need to look no further than Exodus 20 and the Ten Commandments to see this again. Nobody likes to be lied to, and it shouldn't matter if it is at the dinner table, a card table, or a Starbucks. As a matter of fact, if you lie to a judge, you go to jail. Lying anywhere is not acceptable or approved of, and this includes (believe it or not) our politicians. We don't like liars, and neither does Almighty God. He hates it and tolerates it nowhere.

When I think of "Hands that shed innocent blood," my mind gravitates toward the abortion epidemic, and I believe that qualifies. I also think all can agree that there is never a time where the shedding of innocent blood is acceptable. I can't rationalize the harming of an innocent person, let alone to shed innocent blood.

I guess we could foolishly see a proud look when we make a brilliant point with our words and show off our incredible minds. Say that I lie because I really need that raise at work, and I don't believe that God will meet my needs, although I do live beyond my means. So I lie about my kid needing braces and my wife's operation. But to shed innocent blood? Never. We hate it, and God hates it.

"A heart that devises wicked plans" is a basic enough thought if we would consider that any plan not from God is wicked. I hope we don't try to rationalize what a wicked plan is. Yes, a wicked plan is when a person decides to rob a convenience store at gun point, and yes, a plan to become the next Walter White from *Breaking Bad* and sell drugs is a wicked plan. However, have you considered that when a person picks up the telephone to call a friend to gossip, that is also a wicked plan? Any plan that is not a plan of God can be a wicked plan.

There are many ways to devise wicked plans. One is to exchange right for wrong. Isaiah said, "Woe to those who call evil good, and good evil; who substitute darkness for light and light for darkness" (Isa. 5:20). In our world today, virtues such as virginity and fidelity in marriage are branded as old-fashioned and out of touch, whereas promiscuity and adultery are considered contemporary and liberating. "Therefore, to him who knows to do good and does not do it, to him it is sin" (James 4:17). Knowing to do right but not doing it can be seen as a wicked plan before God's eyes.

Please take a moment to consider that it is a heart that is in the middle of the plan. It is the choice and intention of a person to do a wicked thing. It is never an accident to plan to do a wicked thing, and to do a wicked thing is not a reflex action to the situation. It is a matter of the heart, a choice.

"Feet that are swift in running to evil." I think we can all imagine the person who can't wait until Friday afternoon at 5:00 p.m. to start the weekend in some pub.

"A false witness who speaks lies." we see that God mentions lying twice. This must be one of His pet peeves to have to remind us twice to watch what we say. We can think of a courtroom where a person deliberately lies and then becomes a false witness. This, to me at least, falls under the gossip category when a person does more than lie and becomes a false witness who lies. A false witness begins the falsehood with a simple statement: "Guess what I heard?" You are now a false witness.

What about the seventh thing? What does God see as an abomination to Him? It is this: "one who sows discord among brethren." God says that He hate a proud look, lying people, hands that shed innocent blood, a wicked heart, and feet that run to evil. He hates these things everywhere the breath of life is drawn. He hates these things in the world and everywhere under heaven. But wait—when you do these things in His church, He finds this abominable!

Sure, He hates lying and gossip anywhere, but when you bring this in the church, this is the ugliest thing you can do. Yes, God says there are six things He hates, and there are other things in scripture He hates. He hates them everywhere. But when you bring your arrogant feet into His church and sow discord among His people, He finds this more grievous. This is not just bad—it is ugly. Do not bring the common sins of the world into the church of Jesus Christ and sow discord among His elect.

Paul said in Romans 16:17, "Now I urge you, brethren, note those who cause divisions and offenses, contrary to the doctrine which you learned, and avoid them." Those who cause division and offenses are the ones who sow discord among the brethren, and Paul says to get rid of them. They have no place in church, and God finds this an abomination.

God finds it ugly when we as followers of Christ don't love each other.

> Love is patient ... kind ... not jealous ... does not brag ... is not arrogant, does not act unbecomingly ... does not seek its own, is not provoked, does not take into account a wrong suffered, does not rejoice in unrighteousness, but rejoices with the truth; bears all things, believes all things, hopes all things, endures all things. (1 Cor. 13:4–7)

If we were to be so bold as to treat the church of Jesus Christ this way, with love, how could we possibly sow discord among our brethren?

Chapter 11

What Now?

My dad grew up in Big Mud Creek, Kentucky, and the first real vacation I remember taking was to Big Mud to be introduced to his relatives. Going from living just outside Detroit to the hills of Kentucky was a shock to a seven-year-old boy.

This one-week trip brought a lot of firsts for me. This was the first time that I had seen a live chicken up close. It was the first time I saw a donkey, and it was the first time I ever used an outhouse. There are just some things you see for the first time and never forget.

The insects were plentiful, with the mayflies and mosquitoes seeming to have flight control numbers stencils on their bodies as they relentlessly dive-bombed us. The fireflies were out in force as well, and although we had a derelict firefly occasionally in Ecorse, Michigan, my hometown, I will never forget the fireflies in the hills of Big Mud in the summer of 1965.

I found catching the lighting bugs very easy as they floated in the evening dusk effortlessly. As I caught them, I secured them in a small jar once used for mayonnaise. The jar was small and cramped, and I thought at the time that I must have put at least a thousand fireflies in the jar, but in truth it was probably a dozen.

I must have fancied myself a junior scientist, studying the bugs at great length. As the evening dusk grew to darkness, I found that seeking a dark place to allow the fireflies to light up the vast Kentucky sky very energizing. I couldn't seem to find a place in the hills dark enough to hide the light from my twelve newfound friends. Even at bedtime, I managed to sneak the loaded jar past my mother and into bed, and I watched them glowed under the covers until I fell asleep.

I particularly remember the next morning as I woke and scrambled to find the jar, which had somehow fallen off the bed during the night. I recall picking up the jar, looking to my friends and finding that only one had a faint flicker to him. To this day, I don't know if it was just their short life cycle, the fact that there wasn't enough air in the jar, or the most likely fact, that when a seven-year-old boy jostles a jar full of fireflies enough, they die. Whatever the reasons, my friends were no more.

That memory comes back to me now, and it seems to come back to me most often when I see my human friends from church and the way they receive the Holy Spirit. When I was young in the Lord, I held on to the Holy Spirit very tightly, and I see many of my friends doing this now. When I was seven, I never allowed the fireflies to live the life that was meant for them, and due to my ignorance and abuse, they became very dim and then died out.

I see this with my churchgoing friends and God. It is like the Holy Spirit is their own jar of fireflies that light their own lives, and they hold Him close, never allowing the Holy Spirit to do what He is supposed to do: use us to light the world. Just as I thought the fireflies were my own personal items, in reality I had trapped them to servitude to my seven-year-old wishes, forgetting that they had a purpose, and that was to light up the evening sky and glorify God Almighty.

The purpose of the Holy Spirit is to build up the Church and glorify God, yet we seem to think that He is either just a subject for study or for my own servitude. We seem to jar Him up for personal use, just for us. And we bring Him out occasionally to use Him to laugh or cry or fall on the ground. Just as the true purpose of the fireflies was never to be held captive for the whims of a seven-year-old boy, the true purpose of the Holy Spirit is not to be held captive for the personal use and whims of any one believer. The fireflies in the evening sky is their best way to glorify the Lord, and the Holy Spirit is glorified when He is allowed to flow through us to others to light the way.

If God was truly in charge of the church, I would be at least second, and church would be all about Him; Jesus, His Son; and the Holy Spirit. To the common unbeliever, that would seem like God is a conceded narcissist, but He has wonderful reason for everything being about Him that has nothing to do with His ego. Job faced the question of who was really in charge, and God had to put Job in his place by reminding him that it was God who created the heavens and the earth, it was God who put the things in the sea and on the land, and it was God who controlled even the most dreadful of creatures.

If God were finally allowed by men to be in total charge, it would be about His truth and how He holds up that truth. It would be about His Word and the power of it. If God was in charge, He would protect us from violent predators and liars of the faith. If God was allowed to be in charge, He would tell us of what He finds good, what He finds bad, and what He finds truly ugly. If we allowed God to be in charge, He would also tell us of His glory and His love. And we would listen.

The purpose for our very existence is because God Almighty has made it so. The Westminster Shorter Catechism has nailed this right on the head when it answered the question "What is the chief end of man?" According to the catechism, the answer is, "Man's chief end is to glorify God, and to enjoy him forever." If we could only grasp that everything is about Him and very little is about us, we could march forward as a group in a church that honors Him.

Everything glorifies God, and we should offer our very lives as willing participants in His glorification. Psalm 19 begins, "The heavens declare the glory of God; And the firmament shows His handiwork," and we should bow a knee to that knowledge. When I read Genesis 1, I see "In the beginning God created the heavens and the earth," and it continues that it was God who said, "Let there be light." It was God who separated the day from night, separated the dry land from water, created the plants and animals, and created man in His own image. It was God who saw everything and said, "It is good." Every time I have read Genesis 1, I have never seen my name once, or the names of PETA, Sigmund Freud, Charles Darwin, the Catholic Church, the Southern Baptist Convention, or the Watch Tower Society. How can I think that I have a say-so in His creation, His world, His Word, or His Church? Our very purpose on Earth is that it is all about Him, our Lord and Creator.

Let me give you an example in the form of a pop quiz.

Pop Quiz: What is the Bible for?

When I have asked this question to people, I get varied answers: "It is my guide to life." "My roadmap to success." "The answers to all the questions." I also get answers to what it *is* rather than what the Bible is *for*: "It is God's Word," and "It is divine truth." Although all those answers and ones like them have validity, they don't answer the question of what is the Bible for. If you want to bake a cake, ask a baker. If we want to find out what the Bible is for, we need to ask the Author, God Almighty.

> All Scripture is given by inspiration of God, and is profitable for doctrine, for reproof, for correction, for instruction in righteousness, that the man of God may be complete, thoroughly equipped for every good work. (2 Tim. 3:16–17)

The Bible can be my guide to life and my roadmap to success, and it is divine and the Word of God. However, it has to have a direct purpose initiated by God to glorify Himself. This passage in 2 Timothy is very much common sense. The Word of God is profitable for doctrine, and our opinion of what it means has no profit to it (remember about adding to or taking from?). The Psalmist tells us, "Your word is a lamp to my feet And a light to my path," and it is the Word that shows us where we are and where we are going (Ps. 119:105). The Bible is profitable for the doctrine we follow, not church traditions or religious experiences. We have to set aside (or at the least verify) what we are taught on our street corners and search the scriptures (Acts 17:11) to see whether our local church doctrine follows the Bible. This is the only way we are sure that we are true disciples (Lev. 22:31; John 14:15).

We do not and cannot glorify God by following any opinions of men. "Indeed, let God be true but every man a liar" (Rom. 3:4). If we are here to glorify God, then we should know what He wants, and the only way to do that is to go to the scripture for sound doctrine. That, as Paul told Timothy, is what the Bible is for.

This scripture that Paul talks about is profitable for reproof, for correction, for instruction in righteousness, and this saves us from man's opinion of what reproving is, what correction is, and what instruction in righteousness is. God's scripture does these things. Let me show you.

Reproof: We are sinners (Rom. 5:19; Rom. 5:8; 1
Tim. 1:9)

Correction: We need to turn from sin (Ezek. 33:14;
John 5:14; John 8:11)

Instruction: By turn to Jesus (John 3:16; Acts 2:21;
Acts 4:21; Rom. 10:9)

No man, religion, denomination, or building in this world can
have the words to save us. When we follow our men, our tradition,
or our church buildings, we forget that it is God, His Son, and
His Word that save men. The disciples of Jesus faced this question
of following in obedience to Him, and Jesus asked them if they
would like to go away and follow others. Peter spoke up and said,
"Lord, to whom shall we go? You have the words of eternal life"
(John 6:68). The answer? Just Jesus!

This sounds so easy in the common sense department, yet
man has taken charge of the church, and he seems to have God
standing on the sideline while men pick and choose what seems
right for the church. In Judges 17:6 and 21:25, it says, "In those
days there was no king in Israel; everyone did what was right
in his own eyes." That is how forty-one thousand churches are
run today. Each man means well, and each individual church
is caring enough to make decision for the flock, yet each one is
doing what seems right in his own eyes, seeing things through
the flesh and not the Spirit.

If God were in charge of running the Church today, we would
heed Deuteronomy 13:18, "Because you have listened to the voice
of the LORD your God, to keep all His commandments which
I command you today, to do what is right in the eyes of the
LORD your God." That would be the only theme of the Church
with everything being filtered through this: "to keep all His
commandments." The commandments are the Word of God and
only what He has written (not just the Ten Commandments, but
all that He has written).

Remember the rules? Do not add to the Word or take from the Word (Deut. 4:2; Rev. 22:18–19). Remember that God has magnified His Word above His very name (Ps. 183:2). If God were really in charge of the Church today, everything would revolve around Him and His Word. Everything! Even when it comes to the things of Christ. We cannot forget that Jesus said He did not come to change scripture (Matt. 5:17) and that He Himself is the Word of God in bodily form (John 1:14). Church would be about God Almighty, His Son, and His Word, nothing else.

The words of "Change of Seasons" from Dream Theater are bouncing around in my head:

> Oh come let us adore Him
> Abuse and then ignore Him.

When we make it about us and what we want, and we ignore what He has said in His Word, we indeed abuse and ignore Him. We are confessing great adoration with our mouths while the other parts of our bodies do ugly, ungodly things. "This people honors Me with their lips, But their heart is far from Me" (Ps. 78:36; Matt. 15:8; Mark 7:6).

If God was in charge of the Church, He would be giving us a direction to follow, and that would be through His Word alone. God would give the directions, and it would not be open to tradition, change, or interpretation. His words would be given for the sole purpose of His glory being listened to and executed.

Salvation itself is a cry from scripture: "For I am not ashamed of the gospel of Christ: for it is the power of God unto salvation to every one that believeth; to the Jew first, and also to the Greek" (Rom. 1:16). The proclaimed Word of God is the power given us for salvation. It is the Word that tells us that our sins must be forgiven before we can have an audience with God. The Word tells us that Jesus is the only way (John 14:6), and that road is narrow (Matt. 7:14). God sets before us one way to walk, and Jesus is declared to be the only way. It is not always an easy, pain-free walk, but it is a fruitful one.

If we are willing, God will show us Him in every place and situation in life. God has taken me down many trails throughout my walk, and I have seen God in the oddest places imaginable. God has shown me things at work, on long walks, at yard sales, and in the movies. I have to admit something: I'm a Trekkie. Yes, beloved, *Star Trek* has had an impact on my life. Has it changed my life? No, but it has opened my eyes at times.

The android Data (my favorite character) has shown me that sometimes it is best to leave your emotions at the door to better see a problem more logically. And to life, Data said this, "It is the struggle itself that is most important. We must strive to be more than we are. It does not matter that we may never reach our ultimate goal. The effect yields its own reward." I see my Christian walk like that, and I wrote this book with that thought in mind. Our love for others, unity as believers, and efforts alone toward God yield their own rewards.

Our walk with God will yield its own reward, and if we were true to Him and His Word, we would not worry about trying to please people to try to get then to come to church. We wouldn't have to bring in entertainment to satisfy the masses. We wouldn't have to worry about traditions, and we wouldn't have to worry about those churches that are doing things wrong because our church is doing things so right. We would finally all be on the same page. We would simply do things His way because it is all about Him.

Again, I am not saying to tear down the church buildings. There are too many passages about meeting together. Solomon "stood and blessed all the assembly of Israel with a loud voice" (1 Kings 8). James tells us in the second chapter how to treat people "if there should come into your assembly a man," and one is rich and one is destitute. Luke records in Acts 21:22, "What then? The assembly must certainly meet, for they will hear that you have come." David, the Psalmist, and the writers of Hebrews proclaim, "I will declare Your name to My brethren; In the midst of the assembly I will praise You." The writer of Hebrews tells us, "Not forsaking the assembling of ourselves together, as the manner of some is; but exhorting one another: and so much the more, as ye see the day approaching" (Heb. 10:25). And indeed, the day is approaching.

I am saying that we need join together and set little quarrels aside for unity in Christ. I am saying that maybe we need to take the pastor off the elevated perch and realize he is simply a spokesman for Christ. We need the priest to step down from any lofty position and lift Jesus as the head of the Church. We need to have the elders and deacons understand their roles and step back so Jesus can be allowed to step forward and claim His rightful place, and that is the head of His Church as a groom would cherish His bride. We have to step down from the throne of our own lives and turn things over to God.

If we did that, what then? How would we run a church? How about trying this: love.

What are the greatest commandments? Love God and love man. This is where we need to be. The difficulties begin when we pick and choose whom to love. We seem to already pick and choose when to love God (Sunday morning at 11:00 a.m.), and it seems that now the Evil One has us picking whom to love: just our fellow churchgoers.

We are divided into sections on street corners and sealed off by denominational walls, where some are invited in and other are excluded because they don't baptize like us, or they don't use spiritual gifts the way we do. Each believer is stowed away, out of reach from our love, just behind a brick wall of a church.

Although the brick is just a few inches thick, we have made it a chasm that seems miles wide.

We seem to be willing to love other Pentecostals or Baptists as long as they go to our church or *might* come to our church. We are willing to go to a hospital and pray for a church member while walking past a friend we know who is Catholic. We seem to leave that act of love to a priest when we know in our hearts that it is our job.

Pop Quiz: Is God glorified by our division? How could He be?

Paul pleads in 1 Corinthians 1:10 to speak the same thing and not be divided, and we seem to take that as a suggestion more than a command.

This is from one of the devotions I read in the morning concerning love.

> Your love may not be perfect, but it should be obvious. If you're struggling with implementing love in some area of your life, remember these five keys:
>
> * Acknowledge that love is a command (Rom. 13:8–10).
> * Agree that you have the spiritual resources to love others as God loves you (Rom. 5:5).
> * Understand that loving others is normal Christian behavior (1 John 4:7–10).
> * Realize that love is the Spirit's work (Gal. 5:22).
> * Be fervent in your love for others (1 Pet. 1:22; 4:8).
>
> Godly love should be your highest purpose and greatest joy (Matt. 22:36–40). As you love others, you glorify Christ and make Him known to the world. (Grace to You.)

This advice, and our love, is to be lavished on the world, not just a brick-and-mortar building on a corner.

I see church in a different way, I guess. I see the local church building as a type of pizzeria, and all churchgoers are pizza delivery people. We go to the restaurant (church building) to get the food (the Word) and then delivery it to a hungry world. We churchgoers enjoy a dined-in experience a couple times a week, however like all meals, most are enjoyed in the privacy or our own homes with others. We seem to forget that if we eat only once a week (church service on Sunday), we will be malnourished and starving.

Our service to God is an ongoing issue, daily. Our church structures are supposed to be about God, yet we have made them places for men, and we miss the point about the greatest commands, which are love. Paul tells us in Titus 3:9, "But avoid foolish disputes, genealogies, contentions, and strivings about the law; for they are unprofitable and useless". Paul tells us in 1 Corinthians 13 to love and then in Titus to avoid foolish disputes, but we seem to embrace disputes and use them for reasons to form a new church. We are not commanded to dispute and part ways. We are commanded to love in unity.

Let me tell you a story. I want you, the reader, to try to put yourself in this story. We had a power outage due to a massive storm in the area, and many churches were left without power. I had my head deacon, who lives close to the church building, run over and see if there was power at our small country church. He called me back and said, "We are ready to go," because the building we attended had power.

I had talked to a couple of friends from neighboring churches, and they informed me that their power was out in their buildings. I told them that we had power, and I asked them if they could attend our church, seeing that theirs was without power. One said that he was loyal to his church and couldn't attend another. This friend was not Jehovah's Witness, Mormon, or Muslim—he was Baptist, and so was I. Personally, I have a problem being sold out to a building so much that a person would forsake the fellowship and study with other believers. To my friend, church is all about his building, his own personal pastor, his own customized praise and worship, and his own comfort. That seems to rule over sitting with other believers in a different building. He would rather not fellowship than feel uncomfortable.

Another friend I talked to said that they were staying home from church on this Sunday because "We don't often get the chance to lay out of church." This is where I believe most can relate: by finding a reason not to attend church. Church should be a privilege. We sometimes forget that in America, we can attend a church, and we have the legal right to form forty-one thousand churches, whereas in other places in the world, the very mention of Jesus Christ is a death penalty. To view church as something you need a break from once in a while tells me a lot about that person.

When should we attend church? The meeting together of God's people to talk about the things of God should be taken advantage of every chance we get. God is a twenty-four seven person with us, and we repay that constant love by giving Him a Sunday and Wednesday for an hour at a time—and if we get the chance to miss that, we see it as a chance to take a break.

"For where your treasure is, there your heart will be also" (Matt. 6; Luke 12). The question is, "Where is your heart?" If my church experience really isn't totally about God, why should my life be totally about Him? If church is about you, your needs, your fellowship, your praising, and your praying, maybe you do need a break from that occasionally. However, if Jesus Christ is your reason for living, your reason for fellowship, your reason for praise, and your reason for praying, I think you would be with Him and His believers every chance you can.

A Sunday morning power outage would then become a chance to join together in another location. Maybe a church member's home or (dare I say) another church building. Maybe a power outage is a chance to have church on a Monday evening, or Tuesday, Thursday, or Friday.

Church was never meant to be a thing that we do. Let me give a pop quiz to see who has been paying attention.

Pop Quiz: Who is the church?

The answer is Jesus, me, and you—His people. Somehow, we have lost our way by thinking that church is a building where we meet, fellowship, pray, eat, and learn. In fact, you are the church, and you take it with you everywhere you go. For a person to look for an opportunity to stay home from fellowshipping because of a power outage, a headache, or something good on television, that person is one who is asking Christ to leave them alone for a while. I can't think of any time I would ask Jesus to leave me alone. If you can't meet locally for some reason, try meeting with other believers of a different denomination who love and follow Jesus as their Lord and Savior. Believe me, they are out there.

I have many small churches in my area, and some are dying off. There are two with fewer than ten members, and neither has a pastor as of this writing. The church I pastor meets at 11:00 a.m. on Sunday, and I have asked these small churches less than five miles from our building to attend together at our building on Sunday until they get a leader. Both churches refused. I couldn't understand how these good, God-fearing people would rather meet in a building without leadership and without a message. I guess when all you have is brick and mortar, it is difficult to leave.

I again asked both of these churches that if they could change Sunday morning worship time to either 10:00 a.m. or 12:00 p.m., I could speak at their church and then make it back to my building to feed my flock. Both churches refused. What is in a person who says, "This building and at our time, with our very own preacher, is the most important thing"? Can you relate to these stories? Is the building you attend and the structured time you meet more important than fellowship with others and learning God's truth?

Meeting together is supposed to be all about God and Jesus Christ, but we have turned that into church being a private social club that is all about us and our needs. When we have the opportunity to say, "I don't want my needs met today," we find reasons to abandon the wonderful opportunity to meet in the name of Jesus Christ. We forfeit coming to God because it really isn't about Him after all—it's all about us *doing* church.

We have to remember that God is a true gentleman and would never force Himself into our lives or your buildings. When we want to do things our way, either in our lives or in our churches, God will step back and allow us to do so, and He returns when He is invited. He is not a pushy bully, forcing Himself into the affairs of men. At least, not yet (Rev. 2, 3, 20).

I want us to remember that when Jesus came, there were two leading religious groups at the time. There were the Pharisees and the Sadducees, and they divided God's people, Israel. When Jesus came, He ate with sinners, sat with women, healed the sick, and encouraged a religious priest to be born again. Jesus set the standard of unity in a world that was divided spiritually. We are to follow His lead.

I am encouraging unity among believers, not the dismantling of buildings. There are two larger churches in my area, and every Christmas, they seem to join together with a large concert, with the choir being members from the smaller churches. All are Baptist, of course. The question I have to ask is, Why can't we invite the Pentecostals to the choir? Why not the Catholics? Lutherans? Church of God? I am sure all have good singers in their midst.

I am calling out to some to take the first step. Organize a simple weekly Bible study that involves the four biggest churches in your area. Hold one week at the Catholic church, the next at the Pentecostal church, the next at the Baptist church, and the next at the Lutheran church. You get the point. Let the host church mediate the teaching and meet in the name that is above all names, Jesus Christ. Set aside preconceived ideas, traditions, buildings, church history, and everything else that is not of Jesus. Love each other as we are commanded. Acts 17:11 says, "That they received the word with all readiness of mind, and searched the scriptures daily, whether those things were so." This is what I am encouraging.

Maybe a countywide, or as we have in Louisiana, a parishwide choir to perform on your main street at Easter or Christmas. Singers who only requirement is that they love the Lord Jesus Christ and will lift their voice to Him. It is not a Catholic, Baptist, or Pentecostal thing. It is simply a Spirit thing.

The following is from Charles Spurgeon on June 20, 1858.

> Now this great work in America has been manifestly caused by the outpouring of the Spirit, for no one minister has been a leader in it. All the ministers of the gospel have co-operated in it, but none of them have stood in the van. God himself has been the leader of his own hosts. It began with a desire for prayer. God's people began to pray; the prayer-meetings were better attended than before. it was then proposed to hold meetings at times that had never been set apart for prayer; these also were well

attended; and now, in the city of Philadelphia, at the hour of noon, every day in the week, three thousand persons can always be seen assembled together for prayer in one place. Men of business, in the midst of their toil and labor, find an opportunity of running in there and offering a word of prayer, and then return to their occupations. And so, throughout all the States, prayer-meetings, larger or smaller in number, have been convened. And there has been real prayer. Sinners beyond all count, have risen up in the prayer-meeting, and have requested the people of God to pray for them; thus making public to the world that they had a desire after Christ; they have been prayed for, and the church has seen that God verily doth hear and answer prayer.

After talking to a person who has written many books, I asked her what was the most difficult thing when writing. She said, "Knowing when to end it." I find that true because there are so many other things I wanted to address and so many other passages of scripture I wanted to include. I can imagine that if you are a true disciple of Christ, many verses and books came to your mind that you thought I should had included.

To that, I would like to say that there is a passage or two in Luke that I should have included … One also in Colossians … A couple verses in Proverbs and Psalms … Genesis, Ruth, Ezra, Job, Romans … I think you get the point. If you feel I should have included other points and passages, then kudos to you. And you have a wealth of truth and knowledge if you open your Bible. A Bible was never meant to be a paperweight on a desk or something to keep the sun off the back seat of your car from Monday through Saturday. Read it. If God was in charge of the Church, it would be all about Him and His love for us. That is what church should about: you and I loving Him while loving others.

Printed in the United States
By Bookmasters